# TRAVELLERS

# MAURITIUS

**By**
**NICKI GRIHAULT**

**Written by** Nicki Grihault
**Research by** Alan Grihault

**Original photography by** Nicki Grihault

**Page layout by** Cambridge Publishing Management Limited,
Unit 2, Burr Elm Court, Caldecote CB23 7NU
**Series Editor:** Karen Beaulah

Published by Thomas Cook Publishing
A division of Thomas Cook Tour Operations Limited
Company Registration No. 1450464 England

PO Box 227, The Thomas Cook Business Park,
Unit 18, Coningsby Road, Peterborough PE3 8SB, United Kingdom
E-mail: books@thomascook.com
www.thomascookpublishing.com
Tel: +44 (0)1733 416477

ISBN: 978-1-84157-771-5

Text © 2007 Thomas Cook Publishing
Maps © 2007 Thomas Cook Publishing

Project Editor: Rebecca Snelling
Production/DTP/Editor: Steven Collins

Printed and bound in Italy by: Printer Trento

Cover design by: Liz Lyons Design, Oxford
Front cover credits: © Jeff Hunter/Getty, © Jean-Bernard Carillet/
Lonely Planet, © Reinhard Schmid/4Corners Images
Back cover credits: © Olivier Cirendini/Lonely Planet, © John Hay/
Lonely Planet

# Contents

# Introduction

*'You gather the idea that Mauritius was made first then heaven; heaven being copied after Mauritius.'*

Mark Twain (1863–1910)

*With powder-white Indian Ocean beaches and a turquoise sea with dramatic mountain backdrops, year-round sunshine and fantastic hotels, it's perhaps no surprise that Mauritius is referred to as the 'jewel' of the Indian Ocean.*

Dream holidays are this island's forte. Safe yet exotic, Mauritius offers the best standard of hotel service in the Indian Ocean as well as world-class spas and golf courses, top chefs serving mouth-watering multiethnic cuisine and, unlike many tropical islands, plenty to see and do.

The island's key selling point is its beaches, and many visitors can't bear to leave them. It's also a water-sports mecca, with everything imaginable from undersea walks to diving and snorkelling on the coral reef, as well as deep-sea fishing, windsurfing and sailing. Yet beyond the beach, the island's wide swathes of natural beauty have a lot to offer those who want to get out and about. Rolling fields of sugar cane bleached by the sun are interspersed with lush green mountains to climb. There's trekking through inland forests that have soaring ebony trees, home to some of the world's rarest birds. Beautiful flowers, such as hibiscus and bougainvillea and the

ubiquitous red anthurium, fill hotel gardens. As if all that wasn't enough, in the last 15 years Mauritius has developed eco-adventures, which mean

The sparkling turquoise waters of Mauritius

Pieter Both mountain in the Moka Range

getting on a quad bike or in a 4x4, or cycling, horse-riding or even ziplining to explore its green interior. What's more, there are no poisonous snakes and insects or dangerous animals to spoil a holiday, and English is conveniently spoken by people in the tourism industry to make the living easy.

The tourism board promotes Mauritius with the tagline, 'An Adventure of Emotion'. From its swashbuckling history of piracy and shipwrecks, the island's colonial years brought a fascinating fusion of cultures to Mauritius – French, Indian, Chinese and Creole. The people here are also special, giving the island a relaxed, lively and friendly vibe. Multiculturalism informs everything from dress to dancing, and buildings to breakfast. Cultural sites range from colonial monuments and architecture to riotous Indian temples, bustling markets and fascinating religious festivals. However, what visitors notice most is a culture infused with a deep hospitality, where nothing is too much trouble, and the kindness and thoughtfulness of local people stay with guests a long time after they return home.

# The land

*'A garden which some God chose to rest on the sea, Mauritius, where the sea sings and birds sleep...'*

*Paul-Jean Toulet*

*About 8 million years ago, the pear-shaped volcanic island of Mauritius rose out of the Indian Ocean. Around 2,000km (1,243 miles) off the southeastern coast of Africa, Mauritius lies east of Madagascar. Along with Rodrigues and Reunion, it forms part of the Mascarene Islands. These islands, away from major sea trading routes, remained isolated and uninhabited by humans for thousands of years, allowing them to evolve a unique flora and fauna.*

Today, Mauritius is recognised as one of the world's biodiversity hotspots, and much of it has been designated as a protected area.

Mauritius is a decent size for a tropical island, at 45km (28 miles) wide and 65km (40 miles) long and covering 1,865sq km (720sq miles). Its 320km (200 miles) of coastline is surrounded by a clear blue lagoon, mostly ringed by the world's third-largest coral reef. And, in the interior, it can be seen how the local 'Green Island' rum got its name.

Explosions and weathering left the island with crater walls at Black River, Grand Port and Moka. Further eruptions, about 4 million years ago, formed the crater at Trou aux Cerfs (overlooking Curepipe) and the crater lake at Grand Bassin. The last major volcanic activity, just over 100,000 years ago, created the coastal plains. Uninhabited islets that have been important refuges for wildlife are scattered around the coast.

Mauritius is dominated by a central plateau lying at about 650m (2,133ft) above sea level, all that is left of a vast crater, and surrounded by the mountainous crust of the crater wall – three mountain ranges rising just over 800m (2,625ft) from the sea, forming the island's backbone. These mostly velvety volcanic peaks poke out of the sugar-cane plantations that until recently provided the island's key livelihood. The peaks' steep slopes drop towards a mostly cultivated coastal plain and down to the sea.

In contrast, the northern part of the island is a wide plain, and a flat margin surrounds most of the island. The coast is largely bordered by imported *filao* (casuarina) trees, but bleached plains such as those at Yemen (*see p53*) are a reminder of nearby Africa.

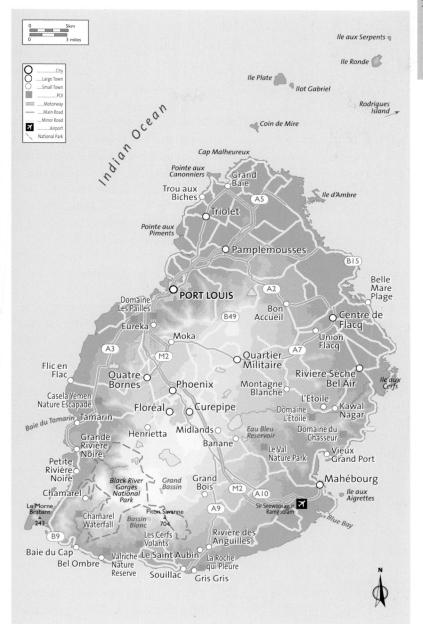

# The dodo

Mauritius' relative isolation led to the development of a unique flora and fauna, including the dodo. The dodo is Mauritius' national emblem and part of the island's identity, although the bird was extinct by the end of the 17th century.

The Portuguese named the dodo in 1500. Identified through DNA samples as a large pigeon, the name may have been given because it cooed 'doo doo'. Eye-witness accounts, mainly from sailors passing through, described the large, flightless, waddling birds as similar to swans, but with none of the elegance. Clues suggest the dodo was grey or grey-brown, with a few black quills for wings and coloured plumes sprouting from its tail. Popular myth portrays the dodo as plump, but in

Wall decoration in Dodo Square, Grand Baie

fact it ran very fast, and the myth may have been based on those birds transported to Europe in a confined space and fed on ship's biscuits!

The dodo's flightlessness developed over millions of years of evolution. It had no predators before humans, and, with fruits and berries, leaves and bulbous roots on or near the ground, it didn't need to fly to find food. It had a strong beak and was thought to swallow large stones to help grind food.

In 1638, the Dutch occupied Mauritius, and its once impenetrable ebony forests were destroyed in order to make way for imported crops such as sugar cane, rice, tobacco, indigo, vegetables and citrus trees. Sailors, invalids, convicts and slaves followed, and the defenceless dodo was an easy target for hunters, although, by all accounts, the meat had a nauseating taste.

An even more deadly threat to dodo eggs and chicks were the rats and monkeys that escaped from ships. They could reach the nests, built about 40cm (16in) above the ground with their single egg. Deer, pigs, goats, chickens, dogs and cats were all introduced to the island, each

A dodo and chick

making life more difficult for the dodo. Slowly, the sanctuary that had sheltered this unusual bird for at least a million years of evolution was destroyed. By 1690, less than 100 years after humans arrived, the dodo was extinct.

It wasn't until 1865 that dodo bones were found, by accident, in the marsh of Mare Aux Songes, proving that the dodo was not just a figment of sailors' imaginations. Further bones were found in 2005–06, the first since the 1920s. There are now plans to upgrade this historic marsh to a World Heritage site, which would include a Dodo museum.

Two dodo skeletons are found in the Mauritius Museum Council in Port Louis, and fine busts can be seen in La Vanille Réserve des Mascareignes, Ile aux Aigrettes, possibly its last resting place. At Casela Bird Park, visitors can see the Nicobar Pigeon, the dodo's closest living relative. Pockets of original forest lie in the Black River Gorges and at Petrin, where you can see The Tambalacoque or 'dodo tree'. However, you will find the most dodos carved in wood, cast in metal, made into soft toys and depicted on paintings and postcards. Pictures of dodos are sewn on everything from T-shirts to towels, and you can even find dodo cocktails, drunk out of a porcelain dodo figurine.

For the full story of this improbable bird, read *Dodo – the Bird behind the Legend* (IPC Mauritius, ISBN 99903-38-15-9) by Alan Grihault, or visit *www.dodosite.com*

# History

**500 BC**    Phoenician sailors from the Red Sea came down the east coast of Africa and visited places in the Indian Ocean.

**AD 900–1000**    Arabs traded along the African coast and probably visited Mauritius. In the Middle Ages, Mauritius appeared on maps with an Arabic name, Dina Arobi (Eastern Island).

**1488**    The Portuguese explorer, Bartholomew Diaz, was the first recorded European to sail from the Cape of Good Hope into the Indian Ocean.

**1500**    Mauritius was accidentally discovered by Diogo Diaz, Bartholomew's brother, when his ship was blown off course by a violent storm.

**1507**    The island was named by Domingo Fernandez Pereira, after his ship, *Isla do Cerne* (Swans' Island), but also perhaps after the swan-like dodos on the island.

**1513**    A Portuguese sailor, Don Pedro Mascarenhas, gave the name 'Mascarenes' to the group of islands that includes Mauritius, Reunion and Rodrigues.

**1528**    A Portuguese sailor, Diego Rodriguez, gave his name to Rodrigues. The name stuck.

**1598**    A Dutch squadron arrived at Vieux Grand Port, in the southeast of the island, naming it Mauritius in honour of Prince Maurice Van Nassau of Holland.

**1638–1710**    The Dutch settled on Mauritius, but only for 20 years. Another attempt at settlement was made, but they finally left the island in 1710, leaving their legacy: sugar cane, deer and monkeys. The dodo was destroyed and the ebony forest plundered.

**1715**    The French arrived and called the island 'Ile de France'. Governor Labourdonnais established Port Louis as a naval base and built a road network. Slaves were imported from Africa and Madagascar.

**1744** The ship, *Le San Géran*, sank during a violent storm, and inspired the 18th-century novel *Paul et Virginie* by Bernardin de St Pierre.

**1797** In the census, the population of Mauritius was 59,020, which consisted of 6,237 whites, 3,703 free men and 49,080 slaves.

**1810** The British colonised the island during the Napoleonic Wars but agreed, unusually, to respect French language, laws and culture, and to allow the French to keep their lands, which they still own today.

**1810–1968** British influence led to economic and social change. Abolishing slavery in 1835, indentured labourers were brought from India to work in the sugar-cane fields, which became the main industry. Chinese and Muslim traders arrived. Communications were improved.

**1835–1936** Indian labourers had few rights, but conditions were improved by the setting up of a royal commission to look into immigration, and a visit by Mahatma Ghandi in 1907.

**1936–1968** Sir Seewoosagur Ramgoolam, founder of the Labour Party, led the fight for independence, which Mauritius gained in 1968.

**1968–1986** Sir Seewoosagur Ramgoolam was prime minister until his death in 1986, and many buildings as well as Pamplemousses Gardens are officially named in his honour.

**1970s–1990s** Successful diversification from sugar to textiles and tourism had a big impact on the economy.

**1992** Mauritius became a republic, although it still forms part of the British Commonwealth.

**2003** Franco-Mauritian Paul Bérenger became the first white and first non-Hindu prime minister since independence.

**2010** Mauritius will become a duty-free shopping haven.

# Politics

*Mauritius achieved independence from the UK in 1968, becoming a republic within the British Commonwealth in 1992. A democratic state based on the British pattern of government, it has 62 members of parliament elected every five years. A president presides over government, headed by the prime minister. The island enjoys political stability, although it suffers from corruption and is unusual in its preference for government by coalition, perhaps reflecting the national multicultural ethos.*

The Mauritius Labour Party (MLP) headed by Sir Seewoosagur Ramgoolam (*see box below*) took over at Independence, and faced problems of overpopulation, unemployment and a mono-crop economy. Sir Seewoosagur established the export-processing zone that became key to Mauritius' future growth through foreign investment.

Independence also saw the return of Paul Bérenger, an extreme left-wing Franco-Mauritian whose aim was the redistribution of wealth on the island. His party, the Mouvement Militant Mauricien (MMM), rose to power in 1982, headed by Aneerood Jugnauth, a Hindu lawyer. Mauritian politics have seen the same figures and families dominate, in different arrangements as multi-party coalitions, ever since.

Cooperating with the private sector turned around the economic crisis through diversification. This was continued by the Labour Government of Dr Navin Chandra Ramgoolam, Seewoosagur's son, elected to power in 1995. Paul Bérenger formed an alliance with the MSM (Militant Socialist Movement), also headed by Aneerood Jugnauth, and, when he became prime minister in 2003, he was the first white, non-Hindu prime minister since Independence. Defeated in 2005, the country is now in the hands of a new party, The Socialist Alliance, headed by Dr Navin Chandra Ramgoolam.

### SIR SEEWOOSAGUR RAMGOOLAM

The most famous and loved of Mauritius politicians, Sir Seewoosagur Ramgoolam is referred to as the 'Father of the Nation'. Born in Mauritius to poor Hindu parents, Seewoosagur trained in medicine in London, England. Returning to Mauritius in 1955, after 14 years in the UK, he got involved in politics to represent the struggles of the lower classes. Becoming a member of the legislative council, he was elected mayor of Port Louis, and at independence he became Mauritius' first prime minister. Pamplemousses Gardens as well as the airport is named after him, and you'll see his picture in even the smallest shack of a restaurant.

A policeman walks past Government House in Port Louis

# Culture

*Mauritius is one of the most densely populated countries on earth, with around 600 people per sq km (0.39 square miles). It calls itself 'a world in one island', and this vibrant multiethnic society of around 1.2 million people is a melting pot of cultures, religions and languages. Mauritians are all immigrants, descended from Indian, African, European and Chinese settlers.*

Those with Indian heritage, who make up almost 70 per cent of the population, are mostly descended from indentured labourers brought in to work on the sugar cane. Of these, around 50 per cent are Hindu with minority Tamils and Telugus, and Indian Muslims, who make up around 16 per cent, came separately as traders.

Europeans are mainly the descendants of French settlers, mostly sugar plantation owners, and are referred to as Franco-Mauritians. The descendants of African and Malagasy slaves, usually mixed with European blood, are referred to as Creoles. Chinese entrepreneurs came after World War II, fleeing the Japanese and then the Communists, and account for over 30,000 of the population. Around 30 per cent of the population, most Franco-Mauritians, Creoles and Chinese are Christian, the majority, Roman Catholic. About 2 per cent of the Chinese population practise traditional Chinese religions, Buddhism and Confucianism.

As 'one people, one nation', according to the national anthem, this co-existence of peoples expresses itself throughout the island. French colonial mansions lie near Indian temples, and the National Store sits next to Chung Choy Snack. It is also seen in Mauritians themselves. Women are as comfortable in saris as Levis, and people as happy eating crêpes and croissants as curries and chapattis.

Ganesh Chaturthi celebration in Grand Bassin

The majority of Mauritians are descended from Indian settlers

In addition, vibrant religious festivals are celebrated throughout the year (*see p18*).

The history of an area partly dictates the ethnicity of a population. Some villages, such as Rivière Noire, have a large Creole population, mostly fishermen, as many left the sugar fields after the abolition of slavery. Floréal and Curepipe both have large Franco-Mauritian communities, and Triolet, with the oldest Hindu temple, a large Indian population. Traditional life is still evident around the island. Women in long boots and straw hats can be seen working in the sugar fields, and fishermen still ply the coast in their wooden pirogues.

## The arts

As an island far from anywhere, it is perhaps unsurprising that Mauritius offers little for the culture vulture. It has limited cinema and theatre, but music and dance are central to this culture's artistic expression, and the earthy African-slave inspired Sega (*see p16*) is the most interesting offering. Second is the colonial architecture, evident throughout the island (*see p50*).

Most of the arts follow in the French tradition. The most famous Mauritian literary contribution, a tragi-romantic bestseller in 1778, is *Paul et Virginie* by Frenchman Bernardin de St Pierre. The novel was inspired by the sinking of the ship, *Le San Géran*, in 1744. Paul tries to save his beloved from drowning, but out of modesty she refuses to take off her heavy clothes. She drowns and Paul dies of a broken heart.

Mauritius' best-known sculptor is Prosper d'Epinay, and his classic statue of the star-crossed lovers from the book *Paul et Virginie* can be seen in The Blue Penny Museum in Port Louis (*see p27*). Contemporary Mauritian artists draw inspiration from other influences. They include Vaco Baissac, whose colourful works can be found in his Grand Baie gallery near that of Francois Vrot, who paints women working in the fields, and there is a host of others.

# The Sega

As far back as 1768, travellers were bringing back tales of the Sega (pronounced saygah), the sensual song and dance unique to this island. It came from the African slaves, who traditionally gathered by firelight on the beach dancing to a rhythmic drumbeat at the end of a hard working day. Now mixed with other influences, the hip movements a little Latin and the hand movements Southeast Asian (and in Rodrigues, the Scottish Reel), it is the national dance of Mauritius. Every Mauritian knows the vibrant Sega, and it is

A Sega party at La Pirogue resort

traditionally danced at family gatherings, festivals and celebrations.

This is a dance of the hips, which sway and gyrate to the pounding rhythm of the *ravane*, a goat's hide drum tightened over a flame and described as sounding like 'a husky bark'. Other instruments that make up the unique musical sound are the *maravanne* (a box – this used to be a gourd or *calebasse* – filled with small stones and shaken like a maracas) and the metal triangle, tapped with an iron rod to give a high-pitched tingling note (originally the *panga*, used to cut sugar cane). The traditional guitar, a single gut string attached to half a dried pumpkin, has been replaced by the more sophisticated electric guitar. Hypnotic and colourful Creole lyrics about the trials of love or the humour of life rise above the rhythm.

A partnered dance, the man stands with his hands on his hips, while the woman shuffle-steps around him, waving a colourful handkerchief, and with arms outstretched. The couple then face each other, holding at the waist and shoulder. To the cry of '*En Bas! En Bas!*' (Down, Down), both bend their knees and lean backwards

Locals play Sega on the beach at Flic en Flac

while continuing to gyrate the hips, ending up on the floor. Perhaps because it was once danced in the sand – although some say it is because the slaves were in shackles – the feet shuffle and never leave the ground. As the tempo increases, the dance becomes more high-spirited and unrestrained and the dancers jerk, stretch and sway with animated movements to keep pace.

The Sega can be heard around the island, blasting from cars or shops, or where Mauritians gather on public beaches. Ti Frére was the island's most famous traditional Sega star, bringing it back into fashion in the 1950s. Traditional Sega, including Ti Frére's most popular track, 'Anita', can be heard at *www.sega.mu*. Many young Mauritians now prefer 'seggae' – a new musical form mixing Sega and reggae invented by Creole singer, Kaya, who died under suspicious circumstances in jail and became a national hero.

If you're very lucky, you may see locals dancing the Sega, but otherwise almost all of the big hotels have Sega performances. In colourful costume, the women with cropped tops and billowing skirts, and the men in loud shirts and pedal pushers, these shows accentuate the eroticism of the dance. Be warned – guests are usually asked to join in!

# Festivals and events

*With a multiethnic population, Mauritius has year-round religious festivals, from the colour and riotousness of Holi to the seriously devout Cavadi. The following is a list of the major festivals that take place on the island. For a complete listing and dates, visit www.mauritius.net*

### January/February
**Cavadi** This is perhaps the most devout and dramatic of the Mauritian festivals, celebrated by Indians of Tamil origin. It is about purifying devotees from evil, and devotees walk to the temple in a trance with their tongue, chest and cheeks pierced with needles and tiny mugs of purification milk hanging from hooks off their backs. On their shoulders is the Cavadi, an arc symbolising the sacred mountains, covered with flowers and with pots of milk, for penitence.

**Chinese New Year/Spring Festival** The most important festival for the Chinese-Mauritian community. They clean their homes, exchange traditional wax cakes and light firecrackers to chase away evil spirits. Chinese dragons and lion dances parade through Port Louis' Chinatown, and red, a symbol of happiness, is everywhere.

### February
**Maha Shivaratree** or 'the great night of Shiva' is the largest Hindu festival outside India. This is when the island's Hindu devotees, dressed in white, make a pilgrimage to Grand Bassin to leave offerings of food and flowers in his honour.

### March
**Holi** Possibly the most spectacular festival is the Hindu festival of joy, held

Offerings to Ganesh

A devotee at Grand Bassin's Ganesh festival

at Grand Bassin. People splash each other with coloured water, throw lurid coloured powder and wish each other luck.

**Ougadi** This is a celebration of New Year by the Telegu Hindus.

## May/June

**Corpus Christi** Devout Roman Catholics parade through the streets of Port Louis.

## August/September

**Ganesh Chaturthi** This is a Hindu celebration of the birthday of Ganesha, God of Wisdom. In Baie du Cap, processions take statues of Ganesh to the sea, and others take their statues for a dunking at Grand Bassin.

## September

**Father Laval Day** People of all faiths make a pilgrimage to the tomb of Father Laval at Sainte Croix, Port Louis on 9 September, his birthday. A French priest who lived in the 18th century and protected slaves here, he is a symbol of compassion and is said to have healing powers.

## October/November

**Diwali** An Indian festival, Diwali celebrates the victory of Lord Rama over the devil as depicted in the epic poem, the *Ramayana*. Also known as the festival of light, it's a pretty sight – with small oil lamps shining everywhere to guide the goddess of wealth and good fortune to homes.

## November

**Ganga Asnan** This is the time the Hindu community bathes in the sea for purification, as they would have done in the Ganges in India. It can be seen at main beaches around the island.

## November/December

**Id al-Fitr** marks the end of Ramadan for the island's Muslims, and is celebrated with prayers at the mosque and with feasting.

## December to February

**Teemeedee** After ten days of purification and praying, Tamil penitents walk across a pit of burning coals in certain temples across the island, before cooling their feet in milk.

### PRAYER DAYS

Hindus have special prayer and vegetarian fasting days on Tuesday, Thursday and Friday; these are the liveliest days to visit the temples.

# Highlights

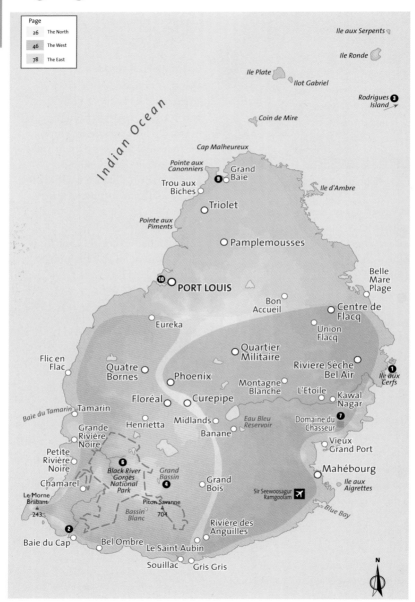

Ile aux Serpents

Ile Ronde

Ile Plate    Ilot Gabriel

Rodrigues **❸**
Island

Coin de Mire

Indian Ocean

Cap Malheureux

Pointe aux
Canonniers     Grand
**❾**  Baie
Trou aux
Biches     Ile d'Ambre

Triolet

Pointe aux
Piments

O Pamplemousses

**❿** O PORT LOUIS

Belle
Mare
Plage

Bon
Accueil     O Centre de
Flacq

Eureka     Union
Flacq

Quartier
Militaire

Flic en
Flac     Quatre
Bornes     Phoenix     Riviere Sèche
Bel Air

Montagne
Blanche     Ile aux
Cerfs

Floréal     Curepipe     L'Etoile     Kawal
Nagar

Baie du Tamarin    Tamarin     Midlands     Eau Bleu
Reservoir     Domaine du
Chasseur  **❼**

Grande
Rivière     Henrietta     Banane
Noire     Vieux
Grand Port

Petite
Rivière
Noire     **❻**
Black River
Gorges
National
Park     Grand
Bassin
**❹**     Grand
Bois     Mahébourg

Chamarel     Sir Seewoosagur
Ramgoolam     Ile aux
Aigrettes

Le Morne
Brabant
▲
243     Piton Savanne
▲
704     Blue Bay

Bassin
Blanc     Rivière des
Anguilles

**❷**

Baie du Cap     Bel Ombre     Le Saint Aubin

Souillac     Gris Gris

N

❶ **Lazing around on Isle aux Cerfs**, an island surrounded by a sand bar on the glamorous east coast.

❷ **Driving along the wild south coast**, where waves crash dramatically against basalt cliffs, and sleepy fishing villages lie along pristine bays.

❸ **A trip to Rodrigues Island**, where the chillis are hot but the people and pace of life chilled.

❹ **Attending a festival at Grand Bassin**, equivalent to the holy Ganges for Mauritian Hindus.

❺ **A spa treatment** at one of the island's fabulous hotels. With so many top names to choose from, Mauritius has become a spa-lover's paradise.

❻ **A trip to Black River Gorges National Park**, the forested centre of the island, and the place to see indigenous plants and wildlife.

❼ **Domaine du Chasseur**, the longest established sugar turned eco-estate, for a quad bike ride and an adventurous lunch of wild boar or deer curry with a stupendous view.

❽ **A helicopter ride** over the island for a fantastic view of the tops of the volcanic mountains, the patterns of sugar fields and the reef from above.

❾ **Grand Baie**, for nightlife, entertainment and shops as well as some of the best beaches on the island.

❿ **Port Louis' Central Market** and the **Caudan Waterfront** to bag a few bargains to take home.

Locals chilling on Rodrigues Island

# Suggested itineraries

*As Mauritius is a small island, it may come as a surprise to some visitors that getting around takes time. With only one major highway from north to south, most driving is along narrow roads, often through congested towns, with dogs and people spilling out onto the streets. Even travelling from the airport at the southeasterly tip to Cap Malheureux along the highway takes 90 minutes, so bear this in mind when you set off exploring.*

## Exploring

As Mauritius is a long way from anywhere, most international visitors come for a week or two, ample time to sample what the island has to offer beyond the beach. The key to exploring is to visit places in the same region,

An old mile post to the capital, Port Louis

doing a chunk at a time. A day or half day is easily spent, sometimes at one attraction. Excursions from the hotel by minibus are the easiest and most convenient way to tour the island, and the most popular option (*see p104*) takes you to both land and sea attractions. Otherwise, options are to take a taxi or hire a car for the day, which allows for more stop-offs and adventures.

## Suggested itineraries

There are interesting attractions in every region of the island, so how to choose? Most visitors head to hotspots in the north, such as the capital, Grand Baie and surrounds; the west for family-friendly beaches, Casela Bird Park, Yemen nature escapade and specialist activities such as diving and deep-sea fishing; and the east regions for glamour, beaches and the offshore island of Ile aux Cerfs. Although with few beaches for swimming there are major attractions in the southeast and southwest, this constitutes off the beaten track, giving an insight into natural, traditional and historic areas of Mauritius.

If visiting for a week, and wanting a general feel for Mauritius, a key place to include on an itinerary is the island playground of **Ile aux Cerfs** in the east – the most accessible and most popular excursion provides swimming on a sand bar, rum punch, a whole range of water sports or a game of golf in one of the world's most stunning settings. As a day or half-day excursion, it can be combined with other beautiful beaches on this coast such as Belle Mare, and perhaps a spa treatment, or at least a cocktail, in one of the island's most glamorous hotels.

In the north, the capital Port Louis and Grand Baie top everyone's hit list.

**Port Louis** has the sophisticated and most traditional shopping as well as main museums and key cultural and historical sites. As suggested below, it's best seen on a walking tour, which takes a morning. It's easy to spend a whole day here, but most people head to **Pamplemousses Botanical Gardens**, which is on every excursion's itinerary. If visiting independently, it's a good idea to lunch at either **L'Aventure du Sucre** or **Domaine les Pailles**, having seen the surrounding attractions first, and visit Pamplemousses later in the afternoon. Otherwise, climb up **Le Pouce** in a couple of hours for great views over the capital.

**Grand Baie** has shops too, but more interesting here are its miles of great beaches all within a short drive of each other, and a whole range of excursions

A flamboyan tree overhangs a road in the north of the island

The Church of Notre Dame Auxiliatrice, Cap Malheureux

both above and below the water. It's a mix of moods from the tranquil northerly point of **Cap Malheureux** which, along with taking a catamaran to the **Northern Islands**, is a place to get away from it all, to the bustling hub of Grand Baie with its nightlife, restaurants and entertainment. Places of historical significance are a little lost here between the sophisticated hotels on quiet peninsulas and the beach bungalows and budget hotels. For those wanting to get away, you can kayak around **Ile d'Ambre** where *Le San Géran* sank or **mountain bike** in a nature reserve.

A catamaran cruise to see the **dolphins in Tamarin Bay** in the west is popular with families and couples. Also in the west is **Casela Bird Park**, another

family favourite, and, next to it, **Yemen**, an African-style savannah and the place to try quad biking or trekking at the base of one of Mauritius' mountains. Being the 'sunset coast', this is also the coast for a sunset cruise.

In the southwest, the main highlight is the **Black River Gorges National Park** up on the uninhabited plateau of **Plaine Champagne**. Most people stop at a couple of lookouts and Grand Bassin, the holy lake for the Hindus that is best seen with a guide. However, nature-lovers could spend a day or half day walking here in Mauritius' largest forest. With limited time, combine a trip here, as many excursions do, with shopping in the inland towns such as **Curepipe** and **Quatre Bornes** en route, dipping down to **Chamarel Coloured**

**Earth**. Hitting the southwest coast, one of the prettiest routes on the island passes **Baie du Cap** and **Souillac** to reach **Gris Gris**, a wild but accessible spot where waves bash against the black volcanic rocks. If you prefer eco-adventure to the more commercial attraction of Chamarel, head to the newest nature reserve on this coast, **Valriche at Bel Ombre,** for quad biking, 4x4 and trekking, or just a great lunch at the chateau.

The southeast is Mauritius at its most characterful. A trip in this region can include a mix of nature and adventure at **Domaine du Chasseur**, a great panoramic view of the coast, and culture and history in **Mahébourg** and **Vieux Grand Port**. A stop-off on the way is the **Ylang Ylang farm**, which won't take long, and while near this coast a highlight has to be snorkelling or taking a glass-bottom boat excursion over **Blue Bay Marine Park**. If there is time and you are a nature-lover, visit the nature reserve of **Ile aux Aigrettes**, a five-minute boat ride from this coast. If you've got a family, the mini-zoo of **Les Vanille Réserve des Mascareignes** further west is a must.

Time permitting, a trip to one of the offshore islands – the **Northern Islands** are the most popular – will give you a feeling of getting away from it all. If you have three weeks or you are on a second visit, a trip to **Rodrigues**, 'the anti-stress island' and a Mauritius of 50 years ago, is a must.

The high street in sleepy Port Mathurin, Rodrigues Island

# The north

*The north has more sunny days than anywhere else in Mauritius, and many of the island's best beaches. It's perhaps then no surprise that it is the tourism hub of the island, centred on the beach town of Grand Baie which has hot shopping, a dense concentration of hotels and the most après-sol entertainment. In contrast, the secluded Northern Islands offer a chance to get away from it all. Then there's the centre of culture, and shopping, Mauritius' bustling port capital, Port Louis.*

## PORT LOUIS

Pronounced either 'Port Lewis' or 'Por Loowee', Mauritius' port capital on the northwest coast is cradled by an amphitheatre of mountains. It was in this sheltered spot with a superior harbour that Mahé de Labourdonnais (*see p10*) founded the capital of Ile de France, superseding Mahébourg. The city is laid out in rectangular blocks, making it easy to get around on foot. Street sellers peddling everything from *dholl purri* and croissants to Chinese slippers stand on cracked pavements in front of the graceful colonial buildings which vie with modern skyscrapers and sophisticated shopping in the Port Louis of today. Mauritius' religious diversity is most evident here in churches and cathedrals, Chinese and Indian temples and a mosque.

### Blue Penny Museum

The first colonial stamp in the world was issued by Mauritius on 21 September 1847, the Blue Penny stamp. Now one of the most expensive stamps in the world, it can be seen here. Mauritius was the fifth country in the world to use 'sticky' postage stamps. Visitors can follow a postal and historical journey through Mauritian heritage at this excellent interactive museum, its centrepiece an envelope with two rare stamps together, bought for US $3.3 million. There's also a good exhibition of art and whimsy relating to Paul and Virginie (*see p15*), and information on the history of Port Louis.
*Le Caudan Waterfront. Tel: 210 8176. www.bluepennymuseum.com. Open: 10am–5pm. Closed: Sun. Reserve for guided tours; audio guides available. Admission charge. Go by excursion, hire car or taxi.*

### Caudan Waterfront

The pretty Caudan Waterfront, built in 1996 on a piece of land jutting out into the harbour which was once home to some disused warehouses, is now the place to find the city's most sophisticated shops and dine within sight of the harbour (*see p152*).
*Port Louis Harbour. Tel: 211 6560. www.caudan.com. Open: Mon–Sat 9.30am–5.30pm, Thur open until 8pm. Good parking and disabled access.*

---

### A VALUABLE MISTAKE

In September 1847, the wife of the Lieutenant-Governor of Mauritius, Sir William Gomm, was seeking an original way to invite guests to their Annual Ball. Summoning a local jeweller and watchmaker, she asked him to produce 500 one-penny and 500 two-penny stamps. Having carefully engraved the stamps onto a copper plate, the jeweller copied the design from the English stamps bearing Queen Victoria's head, then engraved 'Mauritius' on the right and 'Post Office' on the left. No one noticed that 'Post Office' had been written instead of 'Post Paid' until after the invitations had been posted. The mistake made the Blue Penny stamp one of the most valuable in the world.

## Central Market

Built in 1884, Port Louis' vibrant
Central Market (*see p48*) is a
characterful meeting place for
Mauritians looking for tea, curry, fruit,
vegetables, herbs and local gossip, and,
upstairs, a good place to buy arts and
crafts. Lovely Victorian wrought-iron
gates mark the entrance and the food
hall is one of the most atmospheric
places to try Mauritian *gajaks* (snacks).
*Between Queen and Farquhar streets.
Open: Mon–Sat 6am–6pm, Sun
6am–noon.*

## Champ de Mars racecourse

Founded in 1812, what started as a
French Military parade ground is now

### MULTI-FAITH MAURITIUS

Port Louis is the best place to see Mauritius'
religious diversity, and guided tours focus
on this aspect. The white and green
Jummah Mosque has priceless carved teak
doors inlaid with ivory and an elegant spired
dome. The red and gold Confucian Lam
Soon Temple was built in the 19th century,
and near the racecourse are the Shree
Vishnu Kchetra Temple, a peaceful spot
for both Hindu and Tamils, and the white
wedding-cake style Marie Reine de Paix, a
sacred Catholic monument visited by the
Pope. From the Citadel, there's a view
over the Gothic-style Catholic St Louis
Cathedral and the wooden Anglican
St James Cathedral nearby, which was
built in 1828 with 3m (10ft) thick walls to
withstand cyclones.

Items for sale in the craft market at Caudan Waterfront

A mix of cultures in Chinatown

the second-oldest race club in the world. Nestled below the Moka Mountains, it used to be a favourite place to promenade. Now, joining a race day is an opportunity to mix with the locals.
*Mauritius Turf Club, Eugene Laurent Street. Tel: 208 6047.*
*www.mauritiusturfclub.com.*
*Races: May–Nov Sat & some Suns.*
*Admission charge.*

## Chinatown

Mauritius' Chinatown may have lost a lot of the richness of its past, but it's worth a meander along its slightly dilapidated streets to experience its flavour. It's perhaps only in multi-faith Mauritius that the Jummah Mosque, the most important on the island, could be found at Chinatown's edge. Try Swatow Store (*54 Royal Street. Tel: 242 0968*) for authentic Chinese crafts, and the area's most famous restaurant, Lai Min (*58 Royal Street. Tel. 242 0042. Open: 11am–2.30pm*) for a reasonably priced lunch.

*Walking north down Royal Street will take you through Chinatown, which*

### HOLY ETIQUETTE

Tourists should show due respect when visiting religious places. Wear appropriate clothing, not shorts or swimsuits, and remove leather shoes and belts when entering a place of worship.

The Natural History Museum

*stretches seven blocks from Jummah Mosque Street to Etienne Pellerreau Street.*

### Citadel/Fort Adelaide

This sturdy basalt fort, perched on an 86m (282ft) hill overlooking Port Louis, was started by the French and completed by the British in 1834. Unusually, it wasn't built because an outside attack was feared, but because of the enemy within – a French rebellion against the abolition of slavery. However, it was never used. The fort is empty inside, apart from housing the history of the fort, and, upstairs, an incongruous dodo art gallery. The upstairs walkway gives a good overview of Port Louis.

*At the end of Jummah Mosque Street heading away from the harbour, too far to walk, but a short taxi ride from the centre.*

### Government House

Started by Mahé de Labourdonnais in 1738, this elegant colonial building was completed by the British in 1810 and is fronted by a statue of Queen Victoria. Not open to the public, as it's still the centre of government, it is best admired from the top of Place d'Armes, which is opposite.

*Opposite Place d'Armes, at the meeting of Royal and Chaussee streets. Closed to the public.*

### Mauritius Photographic Museum

This museum has hundreds of fascinating photographs showing the history of the island, a collection of old tribal masks from three continents, and photographic and other memorabilia, including the island's first printing press. The photographer-collector who runs it is as interesting as his exhibits.

Pick up a cheap, quick snack from the stalls outside the Natural History Museum and join the locals on a bench under the shade of the banyan trees in the pretty Jardin de la Compagnie (Company Gardens) opposite.

*Vieux Conseil Street. Tel: 211 1705. http://voyaz.com/musee-photo. Open: Mon–Fri 9am–3pm. Admission charge.*

## Natural History Museum

This is the oldest public museum in Mauritius. Opened in 1842, the Natural History Museum's most famous exhibits are its dodo skeletons, the only ones in Mauritius, and one found by a barber at the foot of Le Pouce Mountain in 1900. It's a good place to see endemic and introduced animals, and marine life, to learn about cyclones, and to see local woods, fruits and flowers

A view over Pieter Both

### EXCURSION

**Climbing Signal Mountain**

This hill at the city's western edge takes its name from the antennae perched on top of it. The road to the summit is blocked off to traffic, but it's an hour's easy walk. At 323m (1,060ft) high, this is a great spot to get a 360-degree view of Port Louis. The best time to go is at about 4pm – return as the sun is setting and watch the lights come on over Port Louis.
*Start from the car park opposite Labourdonnais Street, near Marie Reine de Paix.*

as well as coral, tortoises and insects.
*Mauritius Institute, La Chaussee. Tel: 212 0639. www.mauritiusmuseums.org. Open: Mon–Fri 9am–4pm, Sat 9am–noon. Closed: Wed & Sun. Guided tours available. Free admission.*

## Pieter Both

This mountain, part of the Moka range sheltering Port Louis, is named after a Dutch ship captain who was shipwrecked in a cyclone in Baie du Tombeau (Tomb Bay) in 1615. Local legend has it that a young goatherd was turned into the huge boulder balanced on the top of the mountain as a punishment for disturbing the fairies.

### CITY TOUR

If you want to see Port Louis' attractions effortlessly, catch a Citirama coach tour. The tour takes three hours, so still leaves time for shopping.
*Yiptong House, Royal Street, Cassis. Tel: 212 2484. Tours depart: Mon–Fri 9.30am & 1.30pm, Sat 9.30am.*

# Walk: Port Louis

*This walk takes in the main sights of the capital, from its colonial buildings and bustling shopping centres to its religious sites and its most interesting museums. The city is easy to navigate, and everything is within easy walking distance. For the clearest views, less sticky weather and fewer people, the walk is best in the morning.*

*The walk covers a distance of approximately 2km (1¼ miles) and will take a leisurely 3 hours.*

*Park at the Caudan Waterfront and begin the walk at the Blue Penny Museum near the entrance.*

## 1 Blue Penny Museum

Home to the most expensive stamp in the world, this fascinating and well-displayed interactive exhibition on the history of Mauritius has a room dedicated to the history of Port Louis.
*Head into the Caudan Waterfront Centre.*

## 2 Caudan Waterfront

Some of the best shopping on the island, with branches of all the main upmarket shops, duty-free outlets and a craft market.
*Turn left at the pirate boat casino and walk along the quay, past the SSR statue, to take the pedestrian underpass to the right just behind Le Petite Gourmet café onto Sir William Newton Street. Take the first left down Farquhar Street. The entrance to the Central Market is on the right.*

## 3 Central Market

A colourful place to get a taste of local life, have a traditional snack and buy souvenirs at the cheapest prices, if you're a hard bargainer.
*Start in the new market and*

---

**Map legend:**

```
0        100 metres
0        100 yards
★  ...Start of Walk
   ...Police Station
   ...Bus Station
North
N
```

CHINATOWN
EMMANUEL ANQUETIL STREET
DR JOSEPH RIVIERE STREET
Jummah Mosque **4**
JUMMAH
ROYAL STREET
MOSQUE STREET
LEOVILLE L'HOMME STREET
REMY OLLIER STREET
SIR SEEWOOSAGUR RAMGOOLAM
SIR VIRGIL NAZ STREET
EX DESFORGES STREET
RUE LOUIS PASTEUR STREET
RUE LA REINE
CORDERIE STREET
BOURBON STREET
**3** Central Market
SIR WILLIAM NEWTON STREET
Grand Theatre
CHURCH STREET
DUKE OF EDINBURGH ST
PLACE D'ARMES
Governor's House **5**
JULES KOENIG ST
QUEEN ELIZABETH AVE
INTENDANCE ST
Mauritius Photographic Museum **7**
MAILLARD STREET
PRINCE FERRIERE ST
Jardin de la Compagnie **6**
Mauritius Institute
MALLEFILLE ST
COUNCIL STREET
PRESIDENT KENNEDY ST
M2
CHAUSSEE STREET
LEBRUN ST
POUDRIERE STREET
DES ROCHES
Blue Penny Museum **1**
**2** Caudan Waterfront
M2
DUMAT STREET
CHEVREAU STREET
BROWN SEQUARD ST
EDITH
L V DE LA FAYE STREET
MEE BARTHELEMY
CAVELL STREET
Victoria Square
ST LOUIS STREET

Religious icons for sale in Port Louis

*Continue on down Chaussee Street, one of the oldest, to the Mauritius Institute with its entrance in Poudiere Street.*

## 6 Mauritius Institute

Pop into the capital's main museum to at least see the dodo skeletons there. *Walk through the stringy Banyan trees of the Jardin de la Compagnie, before turning left onto Brown Sequard Street and right onto Poudiere Street. Turn left into Old Council Street, which is lined with stunning old wooden colonial buildings. In one of them, on your left at the bend, is the Mauritius Photographic Museum.*

## 7 Mauritius Photographic Museum

This small museum contains an interesting mix of old prints and memorabilia, camera equipment and an old printing press.
*Pass Le Vieux Conseil Restaurant, a popular lunch spot for tourists, on the left before coming out opposite the Grand Theatre.*

*then walk through the old one, coming out on Bourbon Street and heading straight up it to turn left on Royal Street to Chinatown.*

## 4 Chinatown and Jummah Mosque

The pretty white and pale green Jummah Mosque marks the edge of Chinatown, which still has some Chinese shops, restaurants and street names.
*Retrace your steps and walk down Royal Street until you reach a busy three-lane road. The Governor's House building on the left, opposite the statues either side of Place d'Armes, is best seen from this side of the road.*

## 5 Governor's House

This elegant piece of colonial architecture, started by Port Louis' founder in 1738, is one of the most beautiful in the capital.

## 8 Grand Theatre

With a colonnaded front, the theatre is as grand as its claim to be the oldest in the southern hemisphere.
*With the theatre behind you, return by walking straight down Intendance Street, which becomes Queen Elizabeth Avenue. Turn left on President Kennedy Street and right on Dr A Ferriere to take the other pedestrian underpass back to the Caudan.*

# Best beaches

With a turquoise lagoon encircled by a coral reef and 320km (200 miles) of coastline, it's not hard to find a good beach on Mauritius. They really are as idyllic as the brochures promise, with pretty powder-white sand bordering a gentle azure sea. The beaches range from long, sweeping stretches of sand to little coves often shaded by casuarina trees or, at hotels bordering the beach, thatched sunshades, making the perfect picture. Although plenty of activities are available to tempt visitors away from the beach, the beaches are still the island's key draw. Beaches are best known for different atmospheres, sports and activities, and it is worth considering this when choosing a hotel.

Sugar Beach on the west coast

Theoretically, all beaches are public in Mauritius. In practice, purely public beaches are few, but they are not crowded on weekdays. On a summer weekend evening, you may see Sega played among the snack stalls under the casuarina trees.

### Northwest

The largest collection of good public beaches is in the northwest, and will suit those who like a bit of life beside the beach. There is also the largest selection of varied water-based activities and excursions. **Grand Baie** is a beach for hanging out or getting active. It offers an array of water sports including windsurfing, waterskiing and sailing, and, uniquely, parasailing, as well as deep-sea fishing. There are lively après-beach shops, trendy bars, restaurants and clubs. The very popular but small cove of **Péreybère**, off the road between Grand Baie and Cap Malheureux, is backed by a few palm trees and *gajak* (snack) sellers and best visited on weekdays. Many people now head to **Mont Choisy**, a 2km (1¼ mile) narrow white stretch of sand curving north along a turquoise bay from Trou aux Biches to Grand Baie. **Trou aux**

Blinding white sand at Mont Choisy beach

**Biches** means 'Hole of the Does', and it's where female deer used to drink; it is a pretty, white sand beach shaded by casuarina trees. The clear shallow water and reef close to shore make it ideal for families and snorkellers. **La Cuvette**, a long silky beach with clear water between Grand Baie and Cap Malheureux, is one of the finest spots to swim on the island. It's also one of the best for sailing, windsurfing and waterskiing.

### East coast

The breezier coast, this is the site of some of the island's most exclusive hotels, as well as some of the island's most beautiful beaches such as the 10km (16-mile) long **Belle Mare Plage**. It is good for those who love water sports. In the southeast, **Blue Bay** has the island's best underwater scenery for snorkelling and glass-bottom boat trips. **Ile aux Cerfs** is an idyllic small island close to the coast with powder-white beaches and translucent water on a sand bar. With water sports and watering holes, it makes a great day out. There is also an 18-hole championship golf course.

### West coast

The driest, warmest coast with great sunsets, the flat, shallow beaches of the west tend to suit families with young children. The southwest's **Le Morne Beach and Peninsula** is a favourite with kitesurfers and windsurfers between May and October. **Flic en Flac** is a lively beach resort, with a good range of water sports, boutiques and inexpensive restaurants. The shallow waters are particularly good for young children.

## CAP MALHEUREUX

Lying at the most northerly tip of
Mauritius is the peaceful fishing village
of Cap Malheureux, or Cape of
Misfortune, so called because of the
shipwrecks in this spot. It was here that
the British naval force took control of
Mauritius in 1810, although it's most
visited for the pretty red-roofed Roman
Catholic church of Notre Dame
Auxiliatrice. There is a charming view
of the distinctively shaped Coin de
Mire (Gunner's Quoin), named after
the quoin or wedge used under a
cannon, looming large beyond the
pirogues bobbing in the water.

Boats at Grand Baie

### GAJAKS

*Gajaks* is the Creole name for snacks. These
are sold from vans in towns, from a glass case
on the back of a bicycle, in markets, or from
makeshift huts alongside public beaches. Safe
to eat and surprisingly tasty, they're filling
enough for a quick, very cheap lunch.

*Cap Malheureux is reached by the
coastal road to the right of Grand Baie,
by bus, taxi or hire car.
Notre Dame Auxiliatrice. Services:
Mon–Fri 1pm, Sat 6pm, Sun 9am.*

## GRAND BAIE

A small fishing village just 20 years ago,
the deep, sheltered cove of Grand Baie
is now a shopping and leisure paradise,
and the heart of the island's nightlife.
Bustling and colourful, with a cluster of
boutiques, restaurants, bars and discos,
it is referred to as Mauritius' little 'St
Trop', and attracts those who like some
liveliness to go with their beach. Grand
Baie is also great for those who want
action nearby – there is a range of land
and sea excursions as well as every kind
of water sport.
*The M2 from the airport ends at Grand
Baie. It can be reached by bus, taxi or
hire car.*

### GUNNER'S POINT

French cannons can still be seen at Le
Canonnier Hotel (*see p151*) at Pointe aux
Canonniers or 'Gunner's Point', which sticks
out into the sea to the left of Grand Baie. The
Dutch referred to it as De Vuyle Hoek (Filthy
Corner) as many ships sunk on its reefs.

## NORTHERN EXCURSIONS

Water sports, underwater sports and the Northern Islands all lie nearby, as well as eco-adventures.

### Cycling, La Nicolière

*See p108.*

### Horse-riding at Mont Choisy Sugar Estate

Seventeen horses live at these stables conveniently situated near Grand Baie. The 1½-hour guided rides through this 1,700ha (4,200-acre) private deer park go past the remains of the old sugar factory and lime kilns and the estate's colonial home. Groups of up to ten are led by an ex-professional racing jockey. *Mont Choisy Sugar Estate, Grand Baie. Tel: 265 6159. Email: horseriding@montchoisy.com. Rides at:*

*8am, 10am & 4pm. Excursion charge. Drive or take a taxi here from Grand Baie.*

### Kayaking around Ile d'Ambre (Amber Island)

*See p107.*

### Northern Islands

Of the six main islands off the north coast, only Ile Plate (Flat Island), Ilot Gabriel (Gabriel Island) and Ile d'Ambre (Amber Island) can be visited, typically on a day trip from Grand Baie either by catamaran or speedboat.

Trips pass the dramatic cliff face of the wedge-shaped Coin de Mire (Gunner's Quoin), where the beautiful white paille-en-queue (straw in the tail) bird nests. Catamaran trips land on Gabriel Island, connected to Flat Island

Coin de Mire, or Gunner's Quoin

at low tide, when it's possible to wade across. Speedboat trips cross the shallow stretch to trek up to the lighthouse on top for a great view. Trips include swimming and snorkelling and a barbecue lunch on board.
*Croisières Australes, Coastal Road, Grand Baie. Tel: 263 1671. Email: cruise@c-australes.com. Other companies line Grand Baie's Coastal Road and Sunset Boulevard.*

## Round Island

Around 375ha (927 acres), Round Island is closed to visitors while the Mauritius Wildlife Foundation (MWF) works to restore the balance of nature

Stunning rock formation in the Northern Islands

### LABOURDONNAIS ORCHARDS

If you have time, head to the Labourdonnais Orchards where you can hike or mountain bike through tropical fruit trees and swathes of perfumed exotic flowers.

on Mauritius' most important ecological site. It is the only place to find the island's remaining endemic reptiles, three unique species of palm tree and the only place in the Indian Ocean where the Petrel bird nests. Round Island's Burrowing Boa, exhibited in the Natural History Museum in Port Louis (*see p31*), is probably now extinct, otherwise it would be the rarest snake in the world.

## Underwater adventures

For a taste of Mauritius underwater, without having to get wet, or go deep, climb aboard *La Nessee*, a semi-submersible glass-bottom boat that heads out from Grand Baie. Fish swim right up to the glass surrounds.
*Centre Sport Nautique, Sunset Boulevard, Grand Baie. Tel: 263 8017. www.centrenautique.com. Boat departs: 10am, 12.30pm & 2.30pm. Excursion lasts 1½ hours with snorkelling.*

**Blue Safari Submarine** is the only company in the Indian Ocean to offer trips on a semi-submersible scooter of the deep. With two per scooter, passengers must be aged over 12 to ride and over 16 to drive; trips last

Try an underwater safari while you're in Grand Baie

two hours. Its main offering, though, is a 50-minute trip in an air-conditioned submarine down to 35m (115ft), past a wide variety of fish – clownfish, and sometimes turtles, sting rays and sharks – and an 18th-century shipwreck. Ask for a space in the submarine that holds five passengers – it has floor-to-ceiling glass surrounds rather than portholes, one of only two in the world.
*Royal Road, Grand Baie. Tel: 263 3333. www.blue-safari.com. Open: 9am–4pm (winter); 9am–5pm (summer). Trips take 2 hours with transfers. Book well in advance. Admission charge. Parking behind hotel PLM Azur, Mont Choisy beach.*

**Captain Nemo's Undersea Walk** is the closest to diving that a non-diver can get. Weighed down with a lead belt around your waist and a 40kg (88lb) helmet on your head, sink 3m (10ft) under and walk along the sea bed as swirls of colourful fish swim around your face (they're being fed!).
*Captain Nemo's Undersea Walk, Coastal Road, Grand Baie. Tel: 263 7819. www.captainemo-underseawalk.com. Departures: 9am every 2 hours to 3pm. Boat pick-up in central Grand Baie, Mont Choisy and Belle Mare to transport to a platform in the sea; allow 90 minutes (20–25 minutes underwater). Excursion fee.*

## NORTHERN ATTRACTIONS

Inland are the graceful Pamplemousses Botanical Gardens, the island's most visited attraction, and its most modern museum, L'Aventure du Sucre, which gives an insight into the island's fascinating history. Domaine les Pailles, the most accessible Domaine, also lies in the north, providing natural beauty and adventure beyond the beaches.

### L'Aventure du Sucre

This vast ancient sugar mill houses an interactive, modern 5,000sq m (53,800sq ft) exhibition that traces the history of Mauritius. Opened in 2002 in the former Beau Plan sugar factory, imaginative, stimulating and entertaining media such as film, DVDs, talking pipes and holographic images are used to tell the story of sugar through the ages, with details on the cane plant, manufacturing process, and sugar routes and markets around the world. There are fascinating exhibitions on the slave trade, indentured labourers and colonial houses. Children are led through a presentation and quiz by Raj, the Mynah bird, and Floryse, the mongoose. The well-restored machinery is a work of art itself, a mirror reveals the tall sugar chimney, and visitors can walk through the huge vats where sugar was once processed. At the end of the exhibition, sample the 15 types of unrefined sugar served with rum in the Village Boutik. Packaged along with other locally made products, these make tasteful gifts. The museum's restaurant, Le Fangourin, under flamboyant trees, serves a lunch of Seychellois fish, Creole and regional dishes as well as tea, pastries and à la carte desserts.

*Beau Plan, Pamplemousses. Just 15 minutes' drive from Port Louis, off the motorway, 300m (330yds) from Pamplemousses Gardens, parking on site. Tel: 243 0660. www.aventuredusucre.com. Open: 9am–5pm. Admission charge.*

A statue at the Maheswarnath temple

### Domaine les Pailles

Ten minutes' drive south of Port Louis is a 1,500ha (3,700-acre) nature park at the foot of the pretty Moka range. The most commercial of the Domaines, it offers a gentle taste of history, culture and nature. There's plenty to do, including a swimming pool and mini-golf, making it particularly suitable for families. Tour the estate by 4x4, horse or quad bike or take the train *Lady Alice* or a horse-drawn carriage. Other tours include a working replica of an 18th-century ox-powered sugar mill, a functioning rum and essential oil distillery, and the spice garden. It has a choice of four restaurants for lunch and evening meals, and the Italian restaurant overlooks the swimming pool. There's a jazz club and casino here and Sega performances that everyone is welcome to see when groups are visiting.

*Les Guibies, Pailles. Tel 286 4225. www.domainelespailles.net. Open: 9.30am–5pm. A ten-minute taxi ride from Port Louis.*

## TRIOLET

Triolet's claim to fame is the longest village on the island. It has a host of traditional shops and is an atmospheric place to visit during religious festivals such as Diwali and Maha Shivaratree, when everyone takes to the streets.

### Maheswarnath temple, Triolet

Maheswarnath was a lucky man, stumbling upon pirate treasure as he worked the fields around Triolet village. In 1857, with his wealth he built this Hindu temple, the largest on the island, in honour of the Gods Shiva, Krishna, Vishnu, Muruga, Brahma and Ganesha. The design of old temples is far less lurid and ornate than the new ones, and this one is largely white with a few paintings and designs in traditional colours. The statues are perhaps

Take a tour of Domaine les Pailles by horse and carriage

prettiest, with stone carvings of a bull and horse out front and a wooden tiger guarding the temple entrance.
*Triolet Village. Just inland from Trou aux Biches. Open: 6am, all candles lit by lunchtime. Donation accepted. Can be reached by hire car, bus or taxi.*

### Mauritius Aquarium

An attraction for families in the north, the Mauritius Aquarium houses colourful fish found around the island in its five buildings, as well as aquatic creatures such as turtles and octopus (and sharks!). It also has a touch pool encouraging young children to interact with the fish – ideal for those too young to snorkel, and it gives those who can an idea of what to look out for.
*Coastal Road, Pointe aux Piments. Tel: 261 4561. www.mauritiusaquarium.com. Open: Mon–Sat 9.30am–5pm, Sun 10am–4pm; fish feeding daily at 11am. Admission charge.*

### Sir Seewoosagur Ramgoolam Botanical Gardens/ Pamplemousses Botanical Gardens

What started off as the vegetable garden of Mahé Labourdonnais, Pamplemousses is now the third-oldest botanical gardens in the world and one of the most visited sites in Mauritius. Created by French botanist Pierre Poivre (Peter Pepper) as the governor's private garden in the 18th century, it has a huge collection of indigenous and exotic plants from around the world.

Pop to shop at the Comptoir des Mascareignes (*Tel: 243 9900. Open: Mon–Sat 9.30am–6pm, Sun 10am–2pm*), a collection of 25 boutiques opposite the main entrance to Pamplemousses Botanical Gardens that sells crafts, clothes, jewellery, ship models, silk and more. There's also a café and money-changing facility here.

The governor's bust can be seen opposite the impressive pond full of giant Amazon lilies.

Covering 20ha (50 acres) (although originally 100ha/250 acres), this garden of ponds and tree-lined avenues houses 600 trees including one brought by Captain Cook, the curious bleeding tree and a 250-year-old 'Buddha Tree'. Of the 85 species of palm included here, the Talipot palm from Sri Lanka blooms with millions of white and

Royal palms at the Pamplemousses Botanical Gardens

purple flowers once every 60 years, and then dies. Allegedly, one is set to bloom in 2007. There is also a spice garden, deer and a colony of giant tortoises in an enclosure for children. Mahé Labourdonnais' colonial mansion, Château Mon Plaisir, which in 1768 became the home of Pierre Poivre, overlooks the garden and can be visited, as can an old sugar mill. Although entrance to the gardens is free, it's good value to hire a guide to walk you through the lovely avenues, named after governors and botanists who lived on the island, smelling camphor and clove leaves and bringing the plants alive.

## PIERRE POIVRE (1719–86)

Naturalist Peter Pepper was born and died in Lyon, France. Selected by the East India Company to seize the monopoly of the spice trade from the Dutch, he brought nutmeg and clove trees aboard Labourdonnais' frigate from Pondicherry in India. Appointed administrator of Ile de France from 1749 to 1772, he continued and completed the importation of spice trees to Mauritius. His most famous achievement was the creation of Labourdonnais' garden at Pamplemousses.

*Royal Road, Pamplemousses. 11km (7 miles) from Port Louis; car park at the main and side entrance. Tel: 243 3531. Email: ssrbg@intnet.mu. Open: 8.30am–5.30pm. Free admission.*

The north

A guide will explain all the things you can see in the gardens

# Walk: Le Pouce to Port Louis

The third-highest mountain on Mauritius at 812m (2,664ft), Le Pouce or 'The Thumb' is the mountain that most people climb, and a walk up here is as much to say you've done it as for the 360-degree view. It's possible to do the return walk in a couple of hours, but going one way to Port Louis makes this moderately easy walk more substantial and interesting, although you'll need a taxi drop-off and pick-up. Take waterproofs, shoes with a good grip, and a picnic lunch.

The walk covers a distance of about 9km (5½ miles) and will take about 4 hours.

At Moka, turn left at the roundabout towards Mount Ory. After a few kilometres, Le Pouce is signed on the right. After 3km (2 miles), in the village of La Laura, the road bends sharply to the right. Pull in at a dirt road on the left 25m (27yds) after it (GPS Waypoint no 15, South 20 degrees 12.263). Keeping Pieter Both on the right, and Le Pouce ahead, follow the road through the sugar cane, bearing left as the path forks and then narrows. Continue winding around the outer edge of the mountain until after about 2km (1¼ miles) you reach a junction. Take the furthest right of the grassy paths heading up the hill close to the trees, to a cliff-edge viewpoint.

**PORT LOUIS**

0 ——— 1000 metres
0 ——— 1000 yards

⭐ ....Start of Walk
———— ....Road
----- ....Track

N

Port Louis Racecourse
**5**

Le Dauguet Promenade de Santé
**4**

Pieter Both ▲

Port Louis Viewpoint **3**

Le Pouce ▲ 812 **2**

Pieter Both Lookout **1**

*Le Pouce Junction*

⭐ La Laura ○

L'Avenir ○

St Pierre

## 1 Pieter Both Lookout

People often choose to picnic overlooking the distinctive shape and velvety folds of

Walking through the foothills towards Le Pouce

Pieter Both, and so it's the most likely place to spot Macaque monkeys. From here, it's easy to make out the unmistakeable thumb shape of Le Pouce on the left.

*Walk inland from the ledge to join one of the grassy paths heading right to Le Pouce. Pass through a section of indigenous forest mixed with exotic trees before climbing the last steep few metres to the top.*

## 2  Le Pouce

From the rocky top, there's a great 360-degree view of most of the island's mountains – as far as Le Morne in the south and, on a clear day, the Northern Islands to Round Island and the best view of Port Louis.

*Retrace your steps to Le Pouce Junction and turn right, winding around the mountain.*

## 3  Port Louis Viewpoint

With Snail mountain to the left, again named after its shape, and through the trees, Port Louis looks surreal from here. *Continue straight down the path as it gets rocky and narrow and plunges in and out of thicket for about 2km (1¼ miles). When you reach a grassy crossroads at the bottom, turn right and walk on a wide-open path through an avenue of eucalyptus trees.*

## 4  Le Dauguet Promenade de Santé (Health Walk)

Ebony, mahogany and olive trees can be seen on certain sections of this walk, and before the government bought the land in 1881, the owner supplied Port Louis with water.

*Continue straight until you reach the car park, which closes at 6pm.*

## 5  Port Louis Racecourse

The car park overlooks the historic Champ de Mars racecourse, the oldest in the southern hemisphere.

*From here, wind your way down the hill into Port Louis.*

# The west

*Nicknamed 'the sunset coast', west Mauritius is best known for its family-friendly beaches. It's also the epicentre for big-game fishing, diving, dolphins and the only place for a spot of surfing. However, with a sanctuary for rare birds, markets for bargain-hunting, one of the best examples of colonial architecture and adventure in a vast African-style savannah, this side of the island has more than seaside to offer.*

## MOKA
### Eureka

One of the most interesting, well-preserved and striking examples of colonial architecture, Eureka lies in a peaceful but powerful setting, between the Moka Mountains and a deep, forested valley. Purpose-built by British Mr Carr in 1836 to adapt to the tropical climate, it passed through the hands of the island's biggest sugar baron before being rescued from the bulldozer by the present Franco-Mauritian owner.

Eureka is a feat of engineering with its 1,000sq m (10,760sq ft) of wood protected from cyclones and the tropical heat by a wrap-around veranda and blinds, and 109 doors to keep cool. Also typical and particularly pretty here are the turreted windows in its roof, best seen from the back of the house, with the mountains behind. The 14 rooms house furniture from India and China with rattan, suitable for the climate, from

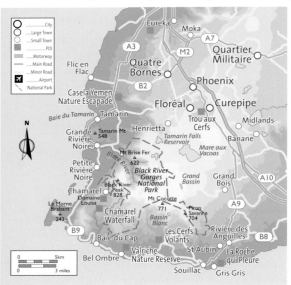

The classic colonial architecture of Eureka

Europe. The baby grand, gramophone and marble stand-alone bath evoke a good impression of life as it once was. Pierre Poivre (*see p43*), who designed Pamplemousses Botanical Gardens, lived next door, and the house boasts visits from British royals.

A traditional Creole lunch is cooked on request in the old stone kitchen decorated with utensils from the 1800s, where cooking demonstrations are given. Gourmet French cuisine with a Creole touch is served in the evening in a beautiful dining room. At the entrance is a small shop selling tasteful gifts and agricultural rum with fruits produced here. Walk for 15 minutes down a narrow dirt path among ebony trees and bamboo to come to four waterfalls on the Moka River

and a tempting natural swimming pool and jacuzzi cut out of the rock. *Eureka, Moka. Tel: 433 8477. www.maisoneureka.com. Most people come on an excursion, but you can arrive by taxi or hire car. Open: 9am–6pm. Admission charge for guided tours; lunch extra.*

## EXCURSIONS
### Island-wide markets
A Mauritian shopping experience has to include a trip to one of its traditional and colourful markets in order to practise the national sport of bargaining. Many stalls move from place to place on different days, but each market has its own character and flavour. Apart from in Port Louis, most markets start early and close by 4pm.

## MARKET DAY

Daily – Port Louis
Mon – Mahébourg
Wed – Flacq
Thur – Quatre Bornes
Sun – Quatre Bornes, Flacq

## Central Market, Port Louis

Built in 1884, Port Louis' vibrant Central Market is a meeting place for Mauritians looking for tea, curry, fruit, vegetables, herbs and local gossip, and it is the one most visited by tourists. The lovely Victorian wrought-iron gates at the entrance lead into an eastern atmosphere and experience. There is the widest variety of local and imported arts and crafts such as *pareos* (sarongs), coloured baskets, linen and silk clothing and cushions, bedspreads and clothes from India, leatherwork and spices.

The food hall is one of the best, and certainly most atmospheric, places to try local Mauritian specialities such as *dholl purri* (pancakes filled with ground peas and served with curry), *gateaux piments* (chilli cakes) or a biriani, and it is now the only place in the city to find the traditional *alooda* (a flavoured iced milk with black seeds that swell up like sago). The indoor section was renovated in 2004 and souvenir stalls added upstairs, but the market has retained its character with uneven pavements, crowds bargaining hard, and fragrant aromas. Start in the new market and then walk to the stalls outside, exiting on Bourbon Street. *Between Queen and Farquhar streets. Open: Mon–Sat 6am–6pm, Sun 6am–noon.*

## Quatre Bornes market

Perhaps the second most popular market with tourists, this specialises in textiles. It is the place locals go for material such as silk, cotton and linen.

## MULTI-FAITH MAURITIUS – HINDU GODS

Small shrines can be found in the sugar-cane forests and by the sea around the island. Hindu or Telegu temples are predominantly red, whereas the Tamils are yellow. The main Hindu gods are Ganesh, the elephant God who stands for intelligence and wisdom, Shiva the creator, and the goddess Durga (known as Kali to Tamils) to protect against evil, worshipped in the temples mid-September to October. There's also Hanuman, the monkey God, who represents power and strength, and Lutchmee, goddess of Light, worshipped at Diwali (October/November). Tamils' main creator is Lord Muruga, worshipped at Cavadee and Govinden festivals.

A road-side Hindu temple

## BARGAINING TIPS

Expect to pay about a third of the price proposed. Start by offering a quarter until you both come to a compromise. If the stall holder still doesn't bite, try walking away – it often works.

The market also sells export-quality seconds, at very attractive prices, with jeans a particularly good buy.
*Stalls are conveniently situated in the town centre. Open: Thur & Sun around 8am–4pm.*

### Mahébourg market
Situated around the bus station and stretching to the waterfront, this is perhaps the most traditional market, and the least visited by tourists. It has all the usual Chinese and Western clothing, and a great one-stop souvenir stall, La Croisée Balance (*opposite

## HAWKERS

If you can't be bothered to go into towns to pick up a few souvenirs and would rather lie on your hotel beach with a cool drink and refreshing swim nearby, don't worry, the shops will come to you. Hawkers are permitted on most of the hotel beaches and sell jewellery, *pareos* (sarongs) and so on. If you're not interested, they'll just move on.

*Monte Carlo. Tel: 637 9766*), selling a variety of baskets, picture frames, dodos and so on for the cheapest prices.
*Mahébourg Waterfront. Open: Mon.*

### Flacq market
Although this is the largest outdoor market on the island, and fun to visit for its atmosphere, it mainly sells fruit, vegetables and other foodstuffs, rather than bargain souvenirs.
*Hard to miss! Open: Wed & Sun.*

The Central Market in Port Louis

# Colonial houses

Most colonial architecture seen on Mauritius was brought by the French when they settled the island in 1715, and it became a blueprint for building by the local population. Cyclones, in particular cyclone Carol in the 1960s, claimed many houses, and many local people rebuilt in concrete. A national heritage fund was set up in 2003 to preserve the remaining historic buildings.

The French adapted their building style to the tropics, and a number of the plantation homes dating from the 18th and 19th centuries have survived. Although many are still private homes, glimpsed through the sugar cane, some have been converted into elegant restaurants and living museums open to the public. Often set in tropical gardens, these are places to experience the refined way of life in the past.

Traditional colonial architecture can be found all around the island. The blue-and-white painted town hall in Curepipe is an attractive remnant of the past, and is open to visitors, as is the Plaza Theatre in Rose Hill, also the largest theatre complex in the Indian Ocean. The police station and town hall in Curepipe, the old school in Vacoas, the courthouse and post office in Flacq, and what is now the Shelter for Alcoholic Women in Flacq are all good examples of colonial architecture.

**Features of colonial houses**

Colonial houses were traditionally built of wood, laid on a base to keep them away from the damp ground and for ventilation. Roofs were originally made of *armagasse*, a mixture for tiles that became as hard as marble and resistant to rain. This concealed a vaulted roof (which in houses open to the public now often hosts a museum) that allows air to circulate. Typical features include ornamental turrets, rows of attic

St Aubineaux, Curepipe

The house at Domaine les Pailles

windows and a roof decorated with lacy wooden or metal fringes, or *lambrequins*, always with a botanical theme. There's always a wide, long *verangue* (veranda), frequently with two gables at the front that could be either open or closed. Eureka (*see p46*) has a wrap-around veranda. Clever touches are decorative pierced screens that look pretty, and help keep the house cool and dry, and doors that replace windows – Eureka has 109 doors! Official buildings such as Government House in Port Louis were built out of brick or stone, although still decorated with *lambrequins*. Poorer cottages were made out of hardwood until the 1960s, when many were rebuilt in concrete and painted bright colours, with the veranda generally enclosed to give the family more space.

Inside the colonial mansions, the design was simple. There were no corridors or vestibules – residents crossed the house through the rooms. The lounge often occupied the whole width of the house, and the kitchen and shower rooms were in a separate building or at the back of the house. The soft blue found on curtains, windows and woodwork inside the house is called wedgwood blue after the famous English pottery. Walls were whitewashed with local lime, and the addition of permanganate gave the shutters their grey-blue colour.

### Five colonial houses to visit
**North**
Governor's House, Port Louis
Domaine les Pailles
**West**
Eureka, near Moka
St Aubineaux, Curepipe
**Southeast**
St Aubin

## CUREPIPE AND SURROUNDS

Curepipe, at 500m (1,640ft), is the island's highest town, and locally known as the rainiest (with 3m/10ft per year). Thought to have got its name from being the place where French soldiers on a long march would stop and clean or 'cure' their pipes, it has a few attractive colonial buildings such as the town hall. Mark Twain may have called it 'the nastiest spot on earth', but visitors seem to like it. The main reasons to come here are to shop at centres such as Garden Village (*21 Sir Winston Churchill Street. Tel: 675 0321*) and Diane (*Tel: 670 4396*), on the way to Plaine Champagne, take a quick spin around Trou aux Cerfs, and visit the Floréal Textile Museum nearby. Curepipe is easier visited on an excursion as attractions are not well signed; even taxi drivers get lost here.

The town hall in Curepipe

### MARE AUX VACOAS

Mare aux Vacoas reservoir is the island's largest lake. Surrounded by pines, it lies 600m (2,000ft) above sea level and is a pretty stop to admire the view on the way from Curepipe to Plaine Champagne.

### Floréal Textile Museum

Floréal is known as the textile centre of the island, and the colourful and modern interactive exhibition here is a fun way to learn about the history and development of the industry on the island. However, the shopping centre here – about 15 boutiques gathered around a garden – doesn't live up to its hype.

*Floréal Square, 1 John Kennedy Street, Floréal. Tel: 698 8007. Email: floreal-sq@intnet.mu. Open: 9.30am–5pm (Closed: Mon). Hourly guided tours. Admission charge.*
*On the main road; come by taxi, hire car or excursion.*

### Trou aux Cerfs

Trou aux Cerfs means 'Hole of the Stags', and the lake at the bottom of this 600–700,000-year-old volcanic crater in Curepipe was once their watering hole. Walking the 1km (²/3 mile) around the rim on the old tarmac road will give you good views over the central plains and the mountains beyond. This is a place to spot local celebs or politicians chinwagging on a stroll or jogging in the morning and late afternoon. An unmarked narrow track, signalled

More colonial architecture in Curepipe – this time at Garden Village

by a break in the bushes and concrete steps, leads 85m (280ft) down to the small lake at the crater's bottom in about 20 minutes; just don't forget the insect repellent.

*Drive up or take a taxi from Curepipe (it's not signposted), following John Pope Hennessy Street, and right into Edgar Hughes Street. Parking at the top just before the road is blocked off with a chain. Free admission.*

## Tamarin Falls

A series of seven waterfalls with a bathing pool below, Tamarin Falls is about 8km (5 miles) from Curepipe, and a 2km (1¹/₄-mile) walk from the village of Henrietta. It's a difficult hike and not so easy to find, so most people visit on excursions, where a guide is provided.

*Excursions or buses from Curepipe or Port Louis, taxi or hire car.*

## Casela Bird Park

Nestled in the lush vegetation of the Rivière Noire district, Casela Bird Park is a sanctuary for rare birds with 140 species of birds from five continents of the world. Its 90 aviaries on 25ha (61 acres) of land house around 1,500 feathered friends, a variety of mammals and a petting farm for children. The star attraction is the Pink pigeon, the cousin of the dodo, saved from extinction. The park serves a simple Creole lunch under thatch if booked in advance. Although not a terribly inspiring layout, it is one of few such attractions for families and it has the added pull of a small safari park with tiger-feeding at 11.30am. *See entry below for contact details.*

## Casela Yemen Nature Escapade

Under the same umbrella as Casela Bird Park, but next door and on the third-biggest sugar estate in Mauritius, Yemen has 4,500ha (11,120 acres) of hills, valleys and grassy savannah, and you feel as if you could be in Africa. Antelopes and zebra have recently been introduced to the 9,000 free-roaming deer, and the property skirts around Trois Mamelles (Three Breasts) Mountain.

Guided adventures include hiking, off-road double-quad, mountain biking and 4x4 rides through 300km (186 miles) of track up and down hills. Wild boar, giant fruit bats, monkeys and moor hens can be seen, and some ebony and teak trees. A 2-hour circuit by quad travels 30km (19 miles). See if you can spot the tree 'Mother-in-law's tongue', nicknamed by Mauritians for its dried pods that crackle in the breeze. *Casela Nature and Leisure Park, Cascavelle. Tel: 452 0693. www.caselayemen.mu. Open: Apr–Sept 9am–5pm; Oct–Mar 9am–6pm. Admission charge. A ten-minute taxi ride inland from Flic en Flac.*

Flic en Flac beach

Quad biking in Casela Yemen

## Dolphin Catamaran Cruise, Tamarin Bay

Named after the Tamarind trees the Dutch planted here, a highlight of this area is a catamaran cruise in Tamarin Bay to see the rare black and long-beak dolphins. Although sometimes boats crowd the dolphins, it is a thrill to see them and some trips allow you to swim with them. Snorkelling and a barbecue lunch on board makes for a relaxing day or half day, and there are great views from the water to Le Morne. *Croisières Australes (Le Morne). Tel: 263 1669. Depart: 9.45am from Le Morne Anglers Club in Black River for a full day on Harris Wilson Catamaran, arriving back at 3.30pm. Trip passes through the* *lagoon around Ile aux Bénitiers before watching the dolphins in Tamarin; barbecue lunch included. Excursion charge. Dolswim. Tel: 258 9821. http://dolswim.intnet.mu. Excursions leave from Island Sports Hotel, Black River. Depart: 8am or 10am, for 2 hours to swim with the dolphins. Excursion charge. A dolphin- and whale-watching half day is also offered.*

## Flic en Flac

A popular and lively beach resort, Flic en Flac is a good place to catch some local nightlife on summer weekends. Food sellers line the shore, inexpensive restaurants and a disco lie opposite, and you may catch some impromptu Sega music on the beach. Local tales have it that the name 'Flic en Flac' came from the sound of the French soldiers' boots squelching across the marshes here, serving as a warning to people poaching deer from the plains. The Dutch called it Fried Landt Flaak or Free Flat Land, and this may have been mispronounced by the Creole population.

### A PLACE IN THE SUN?

Got a spare £750,000? The first island properties on sale to foreigners for the first time in 2006 are the purpose-built luxury villas and apartments in Tamarin. The Tamarina Golf Estate and Beach Club is nestled at the foot of the dramatic Rempart Mountain and overlooks Tamarin Bay. *Tamarina Golf Estate Co Ltd. Tel: 423 8595. Email: obrianb@medinemru.com*

# Walk: The Macchabée Trail

*A mostly gentle walk from Petrin Information Centre, this popular trail heads along a ridge, with great views over the Black River Gorges through gaps in the guava trees. It's a one-way self-guided walk on a well-marked trail that ends at Black River Visitors' Centre near the coast. It is best arranged with taxi drop-off and pick-up at the other end. The trail offers the chance to see rare birds and tall endemic trees, among them ebony. A small exhibition and plant samples identified in the garden are found at the start of the walk; at the end there is more information about birds, plants and the invasion of species. Toilets are found at either end of the walk. It tends to rain a lot here, so take waterproofs with you, and in summer insect repellent.*

*The walk covers a distance of 10km (6 miles) and will take 3½ hours.*

*Start beside the National Park Information sign on the wide dirt vehicle track beside the Petrin Information Centre, step over the chain and continue straight on.*

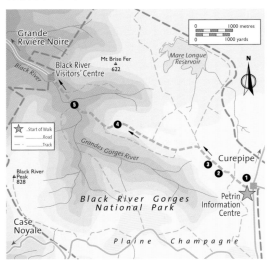

## 1 Endemic trees and plants

The fenced area to your right is where the Mauritius Wildlife Foundation (MWF) has planted endemic trees and plants. This gives a good idea of how different Mauritius looked before humans arrived.

*Walk through an avenue of guava hedges until after 1km (²/₃ mile), marked by a stone sign, you come to a clearing on your left.*

## 2 View Black River Gorges

Black River Peak, the highest point in Mauritius, rises from the hillsides like a little cap.

*Continue straight for 0.5km (¹/₃ mile) until another clearing opens on your left-hand side.*

## 3 Waterfalls viewpoint

Two lovely waterfalls cascade down the gorge. Go a little further for an even better view of them and a moody view of the mountains. Wildflowers are found in this forest with some endemic trees. Mud disturbed by the side of the road is a sign of wild pigs.

*After 2km (1¹/₄ miles), take the left track signed Macchabée Viewpoint/Black River. After 3km (2 miles), you'll get your first view of the sea, to the right beyond the mountains. After 4km (2¹/₂ miles), the road seems to come to an end at the viewpoint.*

## 4 Gorges viewpoint

A stupendous view of gorges either side, and Tamarin Mountain and the sea in front. The path now descends down steps to the right followed by a 1km (²/₃-mile) steep and narrow muddy scramble over roots, hanging on to endemic trees such as ebony, on the way down.

*At the crossroads at the bottom, take the right fork down an easy path, through the gates, and zig-zag on a grassy then rocky path, through eucalyptus trees. Listen out for the Black River and look out for monkeys and birds.*

## 5 Black River

Named after the rocks in it, there are three tributaries of this river to cross before arriving at the Visitors' Centre along a shady avenue of soaring trees, some endemic. The first requires you to wade over a shallow ford. The second is the prettiest, with trees anchored in the water. It's only a half-hour return walk from the Visitors' Centre to the ford, so this scenic section of the path is often busy with daytrippers, and you can swim if you wish.

The Black River

Walk: The Macchabée Trail

# Wildlife on Mauritius

As a small, isolated island in the middle of a vast ocean, there was little opportunity for the migration of animals from other continents to Mauritius. The only indigenous mammals were five species of bats, and only one fruit bat survives today, seen in forested areas around the island.

In the dodo's time, Mauritius was inhabited by two species of Giant Tortoise, along with 13 other reptiles of which five are left today, three of which – the Ornate Day gecko, the Keel Scale boa and the Telfair skink – are only found on Round Island. The tortoises were loaded onto ships as live food and, along with the dodo (see p8), became extinct by the end of the 17th century. The tortoises seen on Mauritius today were brought by Charles Darwin from Aldabra in 1875, and the island now has the largest breeding programme of Aldabra tortoises in the world at La Vanille Réserve des Mascareignes (see p87), where they can be seen at each stage of development. Tortoises have recently been reintroduced to Rodrigues.

The other wildlife you will see on Mauritius is descended from those brought by progressive waves of settlers. The Dutch brought deer from Java (where they are now rare) and pigs (now wild) from Holland. The Portuguese brought the Macaque monkey in 1528 from Malaysia. The *tendrac*, which looks like a hedgehog, and the hump-backed Zebu cattle came from Madagascar.

### Birds

In the dodo's time, Mauritius was one of the richest oceanic islands in the biodiversity of its birdlife, but only 9 of its 26 endemic species now remain, all critically endangered. The Pink pigeon and the Mauritius kestrel are the most famous. Saved from extinction by the British expatriate

An Aldabra tortoise at La Vanille

Ile aux Aigrettes, home to Pink pigeons

Gerald Durrell's Captive Breeding Programme set up in 1973, they are among the rarest birds in the world. The Mauritius kestrel, the island's only bird of prey, was reduced to just two pairs in 1974, but there are now up to 800 in the wild, over half living in Domaine du Chasseur (see p92). The Pink pigeon is Mauritius' largest surviving native bird. There were only 20 left on the island in the early 1970s, but there are now over 360. This bird can be seen in a cage at Casela Bird Park (see p53), semi-wild on Ile aux Aigrettes (see p84) or, if lucky, in the uplands of the Black River Gorges. The Mauritius parakeet, the rarest parrot in the world, was down to 25 birds in the 1980s, but can now be spotted on walks in the Black River Gorges. The other six endemic birds are the Mauritius cuckoo-shrike, Black bulbul, Paradise flycatcher, Grey white-eye, Olive white-eye and a song bird, the Mauritius fody, now the most endangered of all.

### Bird-spotting
All of the birds can be seen in the Black River Gorges National Park (see p60), but other good bird-watching spots open to the public include Point aux Piments, Bassin Blanc (a natural lake), Macchabée Forest Road, Bel Ombre Nature Reserve, Petite Rivière Noire Saltpans, Tamarin Saltpans, and Domaine du Chasseur. Check out their bird song and what they look like on *www.birds.mu*
*The Mauritian Wildlife Foundation (MWF). www.mauritian-wildlife.org*

## THE SOUTHWEST

The southwest has some of Mauritius' most beautiful and varied natural landscapes. It ranges from the unusual coloured earths of Chamarel to the lush forested Black River Gorges National Park which houses the island's largest natural lake. Cradling this is the bare rock face of Le Morne Mountain and an untamed stretch of rocky coastline interspersed with traditional fishing villages, once frequented by pirates, where the fishermen still sell their catch from roadside stalls. The first hotels only opened here in 2004, along with a golf course and Nature Park.

## Black River Gorges

Named after the black stones in the river running through it, this is the only inland national park in Mauritius. It covers over 6,794ha (16,790 acres), or 3.5 per cent of the country, and has the largest remaining and most accessible native forest on the island. Although invaded by exotic species such as guava

### PAILLE-EN-QUEUE

Watch out for the Paille-en-queue (straw in the tail) flying over the tree canopy in Black River Gorges – this elegant white bird has been adopted as the emblem of Air Mauritius. This is also a good place to spot the Mauritius fruit bat.

The Macchabée Trail in the Black River Gorge

Plaine Champagne is named after the creamy white flowers of the privet that grows here. These looked, to Mauritian imagination, like the froth on Champagne.

and privet, Black River Gorges National Park on Plaine Champagne has the greatest concentration of ebony trees on the island, over 309 species of flowering plants and all nine of Mauritius' endemic birds. Look out for the umbrella-shaped *bois de natte* tree characteristic of the island's upland

## TOP FIVE POPULAR TRAILS, BLACK RIVER GORGES NATIONAL PARK

**1 Macchabée Trail** (10km/6 miles one-way Petrin to Black River Visitors' Centre, leisurely 3½ hours). The most popular walk from here, it starts overlooking the gorge and ends up deep inside it (*see p56*).

**2 Black River Peak** (9km/5½ miles return from Petrin, moderate, leisurely 2 hours). Although much of the walk is in the guava trees, the view at the end, from the highest peak in Mauritius at 828m (2,717ft), is worth it (*see p62*).

**3 Bel Ombre** (18km/11 miles return, 4–5 hours' moderate walk). This has the greatest change in elevation of all the walks, from overlooking the gorges right down to the sea. The lower tropical forest is a good place to spot rare birds and bats.

**4 Cascades des Galets** (3km/2 miles return from Alexandra Falls, strenuous). Although short, a good hike down to a pretty 152m (500ft) waterfall.

**5 Parakeet Trail** (8km/5 miles one-way from Plaine Champagne to Black River Visitors' Centre, strenuous). Deep in the forest, this is the place to spot rare and endangered birds.

forest and often decorated with orchids, ferns and lichens.

There are two visitor centres in the park, the Petrin Information Centre at the eastern end of the park on the 737m (2,418ft) forested plateau of Plaine Champagne, and the Black River Visitors' Centre at the park's western entrance in the lower gorges. Petrin Information Centre sells an inexpensive map detailing around 60km (37 miles) of trails throughout the park, varying from shady paths deep in the gorges to the often cloud-shrouded ridge walk to Black River Peak (*see p62*); most start near the centre. A nature trail with native plants has been created near Petrin Information Centre – pick up a leaflet identifying what's there.

*Petrin Information Centre, Plaine Champagne. Tel: 507 0128. Open: Mon–Fri 8am–3.15pm, Sat 8am–11am. Black River Visitors' Centre. Open: 9am–5pm.*

## HIKING TIPS

Plaine Champagne is green because it rains year round, so bring waterproofs if hiking here. Slippery paths can be dangerous – bring proper trekking shoes or boots with a good grip. In summer, particularly, bring plenty of water, sunscreen, and insect repellent if going deep in the forest. Unlike in many countries, there are no guides hanging around offering their services at the start of trails. For guided walks in the Black River Gorges, contact trekking specialists.

The southwest

## Alexandra Falls

Although recently landscaped, Alexandra Falls itself is a disappointing trickle. However, it is worth driving the 1km (²/₃ mile) off the main road through a lovely avenue of paper bark trees for the views across the valley to Bel Ombre in the southwest.

*Signed on the left 4km (2¹/₂ miles) after Petrin Information Centre.*

## Black River Peak viewpoint

One of the most popular viewpoints on the island and on every excursion itinerary, this gives great views north

Plaine Champagne teems with local families picking ripe guavas in March and April. Guava jelly and jam are for sale in shops around the island and make a tasty souvenir.

over the impressive Black River Gorges to the mountains beyond. To the left is the Black River Peak, at 828m (2,717ft) the highest point in Mauritius; opposite, a pretty waterfall tumbles into the gorge. When uncrowded, it's possible to catch sight of Macaque monkeys cavorting along the railings.

*5km (3 miles) past Petrin Information Centre, on your right.*

A macaque monkey at the Black River Peak viewpoint

Bougainvillea is a common sight in the hedgerows

## HORTICULTURAL HOT-SPOT

This island is covered with colourful tropical flowers, 60 orchid species alone, and hedges are a riot of bougainvillea. You may also spot yellow alamanda flowers, flame trees, hibiscus, strelitzia, oleanders and poinsettias. Mauritius is the second-largest producer of cut flowers after the Netherlands, and many people buy the dramatic red anthuriums (from the airport) to take home.

### Plants of Mauritius

Mauritius was once covered in hardwood forest, but these tall, straight trees were much sought after by early settlers who exported them to Europe. When the French arrived in 1715, the land was further cleared for sugar plantations, and today Mauritius has only 1.9 per cent of its natural vegetation remaining, mostly forests clinging to rugged valleys or steep mountain slopes. This natural habitat still supports 700 species of indigenous plants, although with introduced plants and animals competing and destroying their fruits and seedlings, many are threatened with extinction.

The best places to see native plants are Pamplemousses Gardens, Ile aux Aigrettes and the Black River Gorges National Park.

### TRAVEL PLANS

You'll need a hire car, a taxi or to come as part of an excursion here as, being uninhabited, Plaine Champagne is the only place on the island not served by public transport.

# Walks: Cascades 500 Pieds and Black River Peak

*These are two contrasting walks in the Black River Gorges National Park, on Plaine Champagne. The Black River Peak is a popular, easy return walk on a well-worn roomy trail along the forested ridge, gentle enough for the family and rewarded with a unique view from the highest peak in Mauritius. The Cascades 500 Pieds is a short but more challenging hike on a narrow, sometimes rocky, path following the river down to one of the most beautiful, but off the beaten track, waterfalls on the island. A short drive from each other, they can be walked together or separately. Take waterproofs, shoes with a good grip, and insect repellent.*

**Limerick County Library**

## CASCADES 500 PIEDS

*The walk covers a distance of 3km (2 miles) and takes a leisurely 1½ hours.*

*Drive to Alexandra Falls through a lovely avenue of paper bark trees to start this walk.*

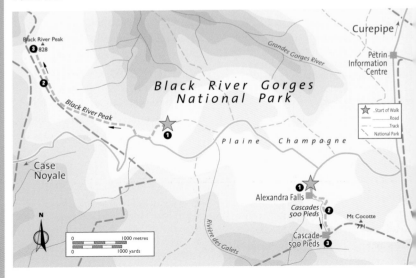

# 1 Alexandra Falls

Recently landscaped, there are paths, picnic tables, and a bridge leading to a viewpoint with an outlook across the valley to the sea near Bel Ombre in the south, and this small falls to the left.
*Walk to the left of the small bridge to the top of the falls and cross on the stepping stones over the small river. Follow the narrow path at the other side as it twists down the left-hand side of the river.*

# 2 View and listen

The path opens out in places to give excellent views, and small streams criss-cross it. Stop and listen to the birds and the distant sound of the river.
*Continue for about half an hour to reach the falls.*

# 3 Cascades 500 Pieds

On the right-hand side of the falls, which tumble down 152m (500ft), carefully crawl forward to look over a cliff face. It is difficult to photograph, so take in what you see and remember.
*Retrace your steps back to the car park.*

Entrance to the Black River Peak walk

# BLACK RIVER PEAK

*The walk covers a distance of 9km (5½ miles) and takes 3 hours.*

*To start the walk, park the car, if driving, at the Black River Peak car park. It's then a short distance along the road to the start of the clearly marked footpath.*

# 1 Black River Peak viewpoint

This faces north over the gorge and beyond to many of Mauritius' mountains, making it one of the most popular viewpoints on the island. Picnic tables, and vans selling drinks and snacks, make it a good place to begin and end the walk.
*The gently undulating path passes through a forest of mainly leafy green privet and guava, too thick and high to see any views but with just enough roots and rocks to make it interesting.*

# 2 Almost there

Just before reaching the peak, there is a clearing and a steep walk uphill that seems as though you've made it. But continue on.
*Walk another ten minutes, and scramble up rocks at the end to reach the top of the peak.*

# 3 Black River Peak

You're rewarded with a unique view of the southwest coast, including Le Morne Brabant, Chamarel, Ile aux Bénitiers and Tamarin mountain.
*Return the way you came.*

## Baie du Cap

It's the dramatic road winding beside pristine bays before travelling under rocky overhangs and past lush hillsides around the river just before Baie du Cap that makes this place memorable. Climb onto the rocky outcrop at the river mouth for the best view of one of the most dramatic roads on the coast. The contemporary Matthew Flinders Memorial, sculpted out of copper, lies just after it. Before the road was built around the river in 1930, couples had to wade across to marry at the chapel on the other side.

*Approach from Le Morne to get the best views (see p68). Park at the Matthew Flinders Memorial to explore the area.*

## Chamarel

Here, nature has conspired to produce seven coloured furrows of volcanic ash in bizarre shades of pink, purple, orange and grey. Caused by oxygenation of minerals, no matter how much the earth moves they always settle back into separate colours – proved by mixing the earth in a test tube. The dramatic Chamarel Falls,

---

### PIRATE LIFE

The small rocky island of Ilot Sancho in Baie du Jacotet near Bel Ombre has a ship's anchor embedded in the coral, a possible treasure sign left by pirates. There is evidence of past pirate activity on the other side of the present main road – piles of coral, fired to make it more resistant to weathering. Is treasure still here, buried beneath the sugar cane?

---

plunging 100m (328ft) over a cliff ledge, are the island's highest. Some people may find this more impressive than the Coloured Earth, a short walk away, viewed from a wooden platform and best seen in the late afternoon. Still, curiosity and the promise of a lunch at one of the rustic table d'hôte restaurants in Chamarel village, 4km (2½ miles) away, lures most people here. Chamarel is one

---

### MATTHEW FLINDERS

Returning home after a two-year voyage of discovery in 1803, British explorer Matthew Flinders stopped off at Baie du Cap only to be arrested and detained as a spy for six years by the French governor. Flinders is most famous for mapping the coastline of Australia. His book, *A Voyage to Terra Australis*, was published in 1814, just a day before he died.

Chamarel Falls, Mauritius' highest waterfall

The bizarre Coloured Earth at Chamarel

of the few places in Mauritius with restaurants serving home-cooked Mauritian dishes such as Octopus Vindaloo, many in unpretentious surroundings. The open-sided semi-traditional Le Chamarel Restaurant (*see p155*) usually attracts the crowds for its great view over Ile aux Bénitiers and Le Morne.

*Main Road, Chamarel. Tel: 483 8298 or 623 5068. Open: 6am–6pm. Admission charge. Many excursions come here, otherwise by local bus, hire car or taxi.*

### Cycling around Chamarel

If you feel like getting active, a half-day cycle circuit around Chamarel is offered by Yemaya Adventures.

*Yemaya Adventures. Tel: 752 0046. www.yemayaadventures.com. Book in advance.*

Mainly populated by Creole villages, Chamarel was named after Antoine Regis Chazal de Chamarel, a French army captain who farmed vanilla, pepper and coffee. Chamarel is still famous for its coffee, and the easiest place to buy some to take home is at Le Chamarel Restaurant (*see p155*).

### Grand Bassin

One of only two natural lakes in Mauritius, Grand Bassin, in the crater of an extinct volcano on Plaine Champagne, is Mauritian Hindus' most sacred site. It's known as Ganga Talao (Lake of the Ganges) locally, and Hindus believe it sprang from drops of water from the holy River Ganges in India. In 1972, sacred water from the Ganges was poured into it and candy-coloured shrines and temples built on its banks. As a pilgrimage site for thousands of Mauritian Hindus, who walk here during the Maha Shivaratree festival or 'the great night of Shiva', it is best visited during a festival (*see p18*). Nevertheless, on any day devotees can be seen lighting incense in a coconut shell and leaving offerings of fruit and flowers on the many platforms around the lake. The newest addition is a Shiva statue, 33m (108ft) high to represent Shiva's 108 names. You can visit independently to see the Shiva Lingham, the burning throat of Shiva symbolised by a stone, and stroll up to the Hanuman (the monkey God) temple, but a tour will bring the Hindu mythology alive, as there is no written explanation.

A pink temple at Grand Bassin

## SHIVA'S JEALOUSY

According to Hindu tradition, unmarried women shouldn't worship Shiva as he tends to get possessive, undermining their chances of marriage.

### Le Morne Brabant

Referred to as Le Morne for short, this bare, rocky mountain is Mauritius' mini-answer to South Africa's table-top mountain with its completely flat top. In a remote part of the island, not too far from the first settlement in the southeast, this is where runaway slaves lived and hid in caves in the 19th century. The Dutch called it 'poison mountain' because of the poisonous fish in the sea there. It now forms the backdrop to a row of quiet luxury hotels and an alluring 4km (2½ mile) beach. The mountain is a challenging climb (*see p73*) and the beach is said to be one of the best places for kitesurfing in the world (*see p135*).

*To reach Le Morne Brabant, take the B9 around the south coast.*

### Les Cerfs Volants

Opened in 2004, Les Cerfs Volants means 'Flying Deer', and this is the only zipline (death slide) adventure park in the Indian Ocean. Here, 11 speed ziplines criss-cross for 2km (1¼ miles) over the treetops and above the pretty Rivière des Galets in the grounds of St Felix Sugar Estate. The highest zipline is at 40m (131ft), the lowest 3m (10ft), the longest 160m (524ft) and the shortest 25m (82ft), and the experience

## TRUTH OR LEGEND?

When British soldiers approached Le Morne in 1835 to tell the slaves they were free men, the slaves threw themselves off the top, rather than face recapture. Whether truth or legend, it gave this mountain its name which means 'The Mournful'.

lasts for four hours. It includes cooling off in a pool at the base of a waterfall and a table d'hôte lunch such as rice, curry and paratha. Groups are of no more than 15 at a time and there are no age limits. Hooked up by a harness, it's designed to be relaxing (!), with little walking in between. The guides are well trained by a Via Ferrata expert. A nine-target archery course is also offered, with compact bows, in a clearing in the forest. There is also a four- to five-hour trek up Mamzel Zabet, nicknamed *la dame allongée* (the sleeping lady), in the 1,820ha (4,500-acre) Yemen Nature Reserve (*see p53*) in the west of the island. Suitable for children aged ten and upwards, this includes crossing a Nepalese bridge and a Tyrolean zipline to a swimming hole. Other mountain trekking with an experienced guide is available by arrangement.

*St Felix Sugar Estate. Hire car or taxi, follow the yellow arrows off-road until you reach a car park. Tel: 212 5016 or 422 3117/3120 (mobiles).*
*www.lescerfsvolants.com.*
*Activity: 8.30am–12.30pm, sometimes afternoons. Book in advance.*
*Admission charge.*

Flying through the trees at Les Cerfs Volants

## Parc Adventure, Domaine Louisa

An army-style challenging obstacle course through a 12ha (30-acre) forest shaded by a hill. This is a clamber along a series of rope bridges and nets, balancing along swinging logs through the trees. It should take around two hours if the adventure track is also included, flying through the forest on ziplines. Lunch is offered after exertions, although you may prefer to head to one of the restaurants at Chamarel nearby.

*Domaine Louisa. About 2km (1¼ miles) from Chamarel Coloured Earth. Tel: 234 5385/727 0869 (mobiles).*

### BEL OMBRE

Bel Ombre means 'Beautiful Shadows', and the restored sugar factory from this estate lies at the entrance to the hotels along the wild and desolate, but inviting, beach there.

*www.parc-adventure.com.*
*Open: 9.30am–4pm. Bookings only.*
*Children aged six years and up (but best aged 12 and up). Bring insect repellent.*
*Admission charge.*

## Valriche Nature Reserve, Domaine de Bel Ombre

One of the newest big developments, this 1,012ha (2,500-acre) nature reserve

A tricky obstacle at Parc Adventure, Domaine Louisa

## THE TREVESSA

When the British steamer the *Trevessa* sank in 1923 almost 3,000km (2,000 miles) from Mauritius, it seemed unlikely that there would be any survivors. However, 16 men survived 25 days at sea in a lifeboat which eventually landed at St Martin, near Bel Ombre. A monument marking the event lies near the old quay.

## CASUARINAS

Much of Mauritius' coast is bordered by Australian native casuarina (*filao*) trees planted in the 1930s. These look attractive, but leave the sandy soil acidic and unsuitable for other vegetation, and they drop sharp cones that litter the beaches. Since 2001, however, they have gradually been replaced by endemic coastal trees.

The southwest

Two-seater quad bikes at Valriche Nature Reserve

in a building dating back to the early 1800s. If you fancy a picnic in the hills, enjoy a day trip that includes one hour on quad bikes, one hour trekking to the waterfall, and lunch.
*Domaine de Bel Ombre. Tel: 623 5615/729 4498 (mobile).*
*www.domainedebelombre.mu.*
*Quad and 4x4: 9.15am–12.15am & 1.15am–4.15pm.*
*Trekking: 8.30am–11am. Full day: 10am–3.30pm. Book in advance for activities and restaurant. Admission charge. Taxi, hire car or local bus, or if staying nearby, by foot.*

lies adjacent to the Black River Gorges National Park and just opposite the new hotels on the southwest coast. Rent double-seater quad bikes or go on a 4x4 journey from the house with the bright yellow shutters for a three-hour journey into the plains, where deer, monkeys and wild pigs roam, and there is a stunning 152m (500ft) waterfall in the forest. Otherwise, a minimum of six are needed to trek into the undulating hills. A good-value prix-fixe lunch is available afterwards at the elegant and romantic Le Chateau Restaurant,

You can also visit Valriche by helicopter

# Climbing the mountains of Mauritius

Part of what makes Mauritius special is its mountains. Unusual and dramatic shapes poke out around the island, giving it a moody feel. Myths and legends are associated with some mountains, others breathe stories of Mauritius past. Although you won't see it on your hotel tour list, all can be trekked and climbed.

These treks range from an easy three-hour walk up Le Pouce (*see p44*) or Black River Peak (*see p65*), both suitable for families, to climbing the precarious-looking boulder atop Pieter Both or ziplining across a 450m (1,476ft) drop at the top of the bare rock face of Le Morne Brabant on the far reaches of the southwest coast. For most mountain climbing here, a guide is recommended. Some mountains, such as Le Morne, are on private property so permission needs to be obtained before climbing them. Many trails aren't well worn or marked, so it's easy to get lost, and the climbs are often technical in parts and sometimes slippery.

The three mountain ranges of Mauritius include: the Moka Range, distinguished by its unusual shapes and stretching 20km (12½ miles) around Port Louis, from Mount Ory to Nouvelle Decouverte; the Black River Chain, which reaches from Mount du Rempart just below Quatre Bornes to Le Morne in the southwest; and the Grand Port Range in the southeast, stretching 24km (15 miles) from Mount Lagrave to the mouth of Grande Rivière Sud-Est (Southeast). Also in the south are the smaller Savanne Mountains, just above Souillac.

*(The names of operators are given in brackets – see Directory for details.)*

## THE MOKA RANGE
### Pieter Both (820m/2,690ft)
With a precariously balanced head-shaped boulder on top, this is the highest mountain in north Mauritius and one of the most difficult to climb, taking seven to nine hours. It's worth it, though, for the stunning 360-degree views. Suitable for ages 16 years and upwards (Les Cerfs Volants, Otélair Ltée, Vertical World).

### Le Pouce (812m/2,664ft)
*See p44* (Vertical World).

Pieter Both in the Moka mountains

The imaginatively named 'Three Breasts' mountain, **Trois Mamelles** (629m/2,064ft), lies in the foothills. A trail offered by Les Cerfs Volants (15 years and upwards) in the 4,500ha (1,112-acre) Yemen Nature Reserve takes eight hours.

### Piton de la Petite Rivière (Black River Peak) (828m/2,717ft)

*See p65* (Yemaya Adventures and others).

### GRAND PORT RANGE
### Lion Mountain (480m/1,575ft)

This may seem an easy half-day climb, but it becomes technical in parts and the slopes are slippery when wet. The trail leads right up the 'lion's' back to its head for great views over the southeast (Otélair Ltée).

### Le Morne (555m/1,821ft)

Le Morne must be climbed with an expert guide, and has various levels of difficulty. It takes four hours with an optional Tyrolean traverse across a crevasse on a 25m (82ft) zipline over a 450m (1,476ft) drop! (Yanature, Les Cerfs Volants).

### SAVANNE MOUNTAINS
### Piton Savanne (711m/2,333ft)

With beautiful views over the south coast, there is a chance to see the Pink pigeon (Vertical World).

## THE BLACK RIVER CHAIN
## Corps du Garde (780m/2,560ft)

For moderate, keen hikers, a climb up this mountain that looms over the town of Rose Hill affords a view over Mauritius' main inland cities and the west of the island (Yanature).

### Mount du Rempart (545m/1,788ft)

On the west coast behind Casela Bird Park, Mark Twain referred to this mountain as the 'Pocket Matterhorn'. The final stretch is a steep rock climb.

# Drive: From Gris Gris to Blue Bay

*The wild south coast, where waves crash on the basalt rocks below the cliffs, is the least explored region of Mauritius. This drive incorporates short walks from the best viewpoints with unusual rock phenomena, and can be extended to a full day, with an excursion to La Vanille Réserve des Mascareignes. There are few restaurants along this coast, but plenty of picnic spots, so bring a packed lunch as well as sturdy shoes and a light jacket for a windbreak.*

*The drive covers a distance of 45km (28 miles) and will take between 4 and 6 hours.*

*Starting from Souillac, take the road signed to Gris Gris, and park above the cliffs.*

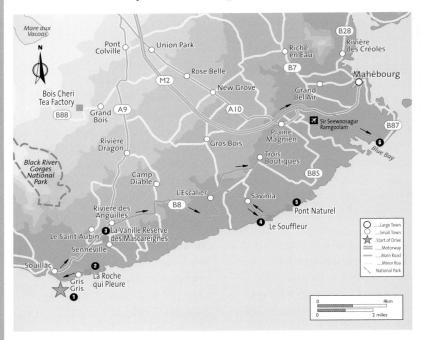

# 1 Gris Gris viewpoint

Where a wild sea crashes over basalt rocks, this is one of the most popular viewpoints on the island.

*Take the steps down to the beach and at the bottom turn left down a small, rough grassy track. A short climb up a bank brings you into a clear track on the top of the cliff among the* filao *trees. After 15 minutes, at the end of the beach is a flat grassy area on a promontory.*

# 2 La Roche qui Pleure

The name La Roche qui Pleure (The Rock that Weeps) refers to the lower rocky outcrop below the promontory, often awash with water. From here, there are great views along the coast. The rock shaped like a hat in the sea, to the right, is said to be the Gris Gris, or 'witch'.

*The path left up the hill takes you further, coming to an abrupt and dramatic end after 15 minutes, where a river cuts through to the sea. Retrace your steps to the car park.*

*Drive on the A9 out of Souillac towards Rivière des Anguilles. Turn right on the B8 to the airport. To visit La Vanille Réserve des Mascareignes, follow the one-way system around the village to the signposted entrance.*

# 3 La Vanille Réserve des Mascareignes

A crocodile and tortoise breeding project, there's at least a couple of hours' worth here for children and adults. There's also the Hungry Crocodile restaurant, a good lunch stop.

*At L'Escalier turn right at the police station, past the Savanna Sugar Estate mill. After about 4km (2½ miles) is the end of the road and Le Souffleur.*

# 4 Le Souffleur

Look over the railings towards the rock in the sea where, infrequently, spray spurts out of a hole at high tide. It once roared 18m (60ft) up through this natural blowhole.

*Walk east, or left if facing the sea, along the path from Le Souffleur. Follow the rocky road and flattened grassy path alongside the cliffs for about 30 minutes, or 2km (1¼ miles) to reach Port Naturel.*

# 5 Pont Naturel (Natural Bridge)

Least known and visited of the tourist sites, rocks have formed a natural bridge over the sea here. You can walk over it, at your own risk.

*Retrace your steps and then drive back to L'Escalier and turn right. Follow the B8 to Plaine Magnien. Join the motorway near the airport and turn left. At the next roundabout, turn right towards Mahébourg. After 4km (2½ miles), turn right towards Blue Bay.*

# 6 Blue Bay

This public beach has the best underwater marine life close to shore on the island. Snorkel, take a glass-bottom boat, or swim from the beach.

Drive: From Gris Gris to Blue Bay

# Pirates and treasure

Although Madagascar and Reunion were most popular with Indian Ocean pirates in the 17th century, Mauritius was also a haven. Close to shipping routes, but far enough away to discourage pursuit, with a rugged shoreline ideal for hiding after an attack, and bays and creeks to stash treasure, hopeful hunters dig even today.

Pirate sites along the coast of Mauritius were left untouched for more than 200 years, but as some pirates died in fights or were shipwrecked, bounty hunters came to dig in hope of finding abandoned treasure during the 1900s. Some got lucky. Menon Prayag, a sugar baron from Rivière du Rempart district, inherited his wealth from his great grandfather who accidentally stumbled upon treasure while working as a poor immigrant labourer. Just a few years ago, a fisherman came across two carved heads stuck in the coral near Baie du Tombeau. These carvings were originally being taken back to Europe on the shipwrecked *Banda*, and were probably washed into view by a cyclone. Fishermen here also claim to have seen the ghost of La Buse (*see opposite*) sitting on the rocks with his sword across his knees, shouting to them that his treasure was buried nearby. One of the Dutch commanders of Mauritius, Captain Hubert Hugo, was once a pirate and, even after the departure of the Dutch in 1710, Mauritius remained a favourite pirate

The pirate influence is everywhere, even in this casino in Port Louis

A 'pirate' ship at Ile aux Cerfs

spot until the French settlers came in 1721 and ended the golden age of pirateering.

### La Buse (the Buzzard)

La Buse was one of Mauritius' best-known pirates. Born Captain Olivier Le Vasseur in Calais in the 17th century, he arrived in Mauritius around 1720, en route capturing a Portuguese ship, the *Vierge-du-Cap*, in Bourbon (present-day Reunion). La Buse continued to plunder ships in the area until 1730 when he was captured. On the day of his hanging, La Buse is said to have thrown a piece of parchment to the crowd, shouting, 'Find my treasure he who can!' On the parchment was a cryptogram showing the site, starting a treasure hunt that stretched from the Seychelles through Mauritius and Reunion, to the southern tip of Madagascar. In Mauritius, treasure hunters dug at Klondyke (Black River) in 1902 and 1912, Walhalla (Black River) in 1925, Pointe Vacoas (La Cambuse) in 1926 and Saint Antoine

(Belmont at Poudre D'Or) in 1933. Is the treasure still there? Nobody knows.

### Buried treasure

There may or may not be any treasure left in Mauritius, but there is no doubt that it was buried here as signs designed to help pirates return to the right spot can still be seen today. As well as documents, maps, plans and cryptograms, the pirates carved signs such as a tortoise, pirate's boot, bull's eyes, arrows, crosses and other inscriptions in rock. Unfortunately, many historic sites are being destroyed by the mechanical diggers of treasure hunters, and Mauritius' history is in danger of being lost. There are currently no organised pirate tours on the island, but look out for pirate signs if you're visiting the following places, mostly in the south:
Poudre d'Or village
Pointe du Diable (Devil's Point)
National History Museum, Mahébourg
Ile des Deux Cocos
Souillac, Ilot Sancho.

# The east

*'Mauritius, a pearl distilling sweetness on the world.'*

Joseph Conrad

*With many of the island's best hotels and a coastline blessed with pretty coves and long sandy beaches, the east coast is associated with glitz and glamour. It's also a mecca for all manner of water sports. Cooled by the sea breeze, which makes it good for windsurfing and kitesurfing, this coast has the country's favourite island playground – Ile aux Cerfs. Inland, it boasts the island's largest open-air market in the village of Flacq.*

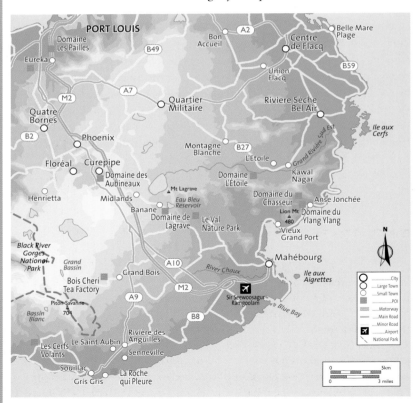

The museum at Bois Cheri Tea Factory

8.30am–3.30pm, Sat 8.30–11.30am; winter Wed only. Drive, take a taxi or go on the Tea Route excursion.

## Belle Mare Plage/Beach

Stretching from Trou d'Eau Douce to Pointe de Flacq, Belle Mare is regarded as one of the most beautiful beaches on the island, although motorised water sports can make it noisy. Off the beach is Captain Nemo's Undersea Walk (see p39) and the Pass, the east's most famous dive site.

*Little public transport to this beach, so take a taxi or hire car.*

## Bois Cheri Tea Factory

The modern Bois Cheri Tea Factory and museum offer a self-guided informative exhibition followed by an interesting and informative tour of the tea factory. Then, a short drive beside the tea fields leads to a DIY tea tasting at a former basic hunting lodge with a panoramic view of the south.

*Bois Cheri Tea Estate, Grand Bois. Tel: 617 9109. Open: summer Mon–Fri*

## Domaine des Aubineaux

Reached through a tunnel of bamboo, Domaine des Aubineaux is a whitewashed house with blue shutters overlooking a manicured garden built in 1872. It only opened to the public in 2000, when the last member of the family died. Everything has been left as it was – gorgeous wooden furniture imported from all over the world in teak and oak, and with items such as a marble stand-alone bathtub. Interesting side rooms reveal paintings of colonial houses now knocked down by cyclones. Tea and crêpes with jam and rum are served in the café across from the house.

*Curepipe. Tel: 626 1513. www.larouteduthe.mu. Open: 9am–5pm. Admission charge; cheaper booked as part of the Tea Route. By hire car or taxi or on the Tea Route excursion.*

## Domaine L'Étoile

The pretty thatched eco-chalets nestling in a valley backed by mountains and fronted by sugar-cane fields were originally built as a film set for *Paul & Virginie* (1972), based on the island's most popular legend (see p15). They are now Domaine L'Étoile's reception and restaurant, where an authentic Mauritian buffet lunch is served. L'Étoile and Ferney, a neighbouring estate, opened 15,200ha (38,000 acres) to ecotourism in 2002. Three-hour quad biking trips visit deer-filled forested mountains with ebony trees, cinnamon and sometimes Mauritian Kestrel. Four-by-four trips travel past coffee and vanilla plantations to Falaise Rouge, a house overlooking Mahébourg with an exhibition on the battle of Grand Port and a view over a string of islets in the historic southeast. Five treks are offered, including an easy, botanical one with over 80 indigenous plants, as well as mountain-biking circuits. The archery course, using traditional bows with 20 targets in a 10ha (25 acre) forest clearing, is unique to Mauritius.

*L'Étoile and Ferney, between Montagne Blanche and Kawal Nagar village. Tel: 433 1010 or 727 1050 (mobile). www.cieletnature.com. Activities & lunch (included): 9.30am–1.30pm & noon–4pm. Book in advance. Admission charge. Note: In hunting season (June–Sept), activities are subject to change. Local bus to Mahébourg & taxi or hire car to get there.*

## Ile aux Cerfs

Named after the stags (*cerf*) that once lived here, this island paradise surrounded by a sand bar just off the east coast is the place to flop or loll in the shallows. Stalls selling *pareos* (sarongs) and surfwear vie with the banana boat ride sellers, but you can still find a calm spot on the sand, away from the boat jetty. This island, among the top sites in Mauritius, is not as small as it looks; measuring around 300ha (741 acres), it takes a couple of hours to walk around it. At low tide, it's possible to wade across to Ile de L'Est, but be aware of the currents and motorboats in this narrow causeway. There are two restaurants on the island,

The thatched roofs of Domaine L'Etoile

of which *Paul and Virginie* is the best for an elegant fish lunch (*open: noon–3pm*). The speciality at the rustic Sands Bar, a great place to hang out in rattan armchairs in the afternoon, is Planter's Punch (*open: 9.30am–5pm; snacks served 11.30am–4.30pm*). For the active, there's every water sport imaginable here, and for golfers, a game in one of the world's most beautiful settings can be booked through Le Touessrok Hotel (*Trou d'Eau Douce; tel: 402 7400; http://oneandonlyletouessrok. com*) across the water.

*Half-hourly ferry: 8am–5pm (last boat back) from the public beach at Trou d'Eau Douce. Weekends, when it tends to get crowded, are best avoided. No admission charge – boat fare only.*

## Le Saint Aubin

This is the family home of Pierre de St Aubin who started a sugar factory in 1819, and the estate surrounding this elegant mansion now produces rum and grows vanilla and anthurium flowers. The table d'hôte Creole lunch in the elegant dining room is the highlight, but there's a museum in the roof upstairs, underneath original beams, and a stroll around the house reveals authentic furnishings and photographs of colonial times.

'Maison du Rhum' is one of the few places on the island to produce agricultural rum, that is, from the first pressing of the sugar cane. See the juice crushed out of the sugar cane and all the stages of production before a

Vanilla is grown at Le Saint Aubin

tasting in the bar and an optional pre-lunch rum cocktail on the veranda. Across the gardens, scattered with wooden benches under the trees, is the Vanilla House with a small film on vanilla production, museum and greenhouse with both vanilla and anthurium flowers.

*Rivière des Anguilles. Tel: 626 1513. Email: lesaintaubin@intnet.mu. www.larouteduthe.mu. Open: 9am–5pm. Admission charge; cheaper booked as part of the Tea Route. By hire car or taxi or as part of the Tea Route excursion.*

### DUTCH REMAINS

Vlak means 'flat ground' in Dutch, and Flacq is the only town on the east coast. It was covered in ebony forest back in the dodo's time. It's now known for its large, lively market.

# The Tea Route

*It takes two days to process tea, three months to mature it and three minutes to drink it...*

Next to water, tea is the second-most common beverage consumed worldwide. A priest first brought tea plants from China to Mauritius, but it wasn't until the 1960s that plantations appeared. Now 40sq km (15sq miles) is under cultivation, mainly in the cooler, wetter, central part of the island. Mauritius has three tea producers: La Flora, Corson and Bois Cheri. The Bois Cheri Tea Factory produces 7,000 tonnes a year alone, and the crop is now second to sugar cane.

The tea plant is a dense bush with deep roots that can withstand cyclones. The tea pickers' art, plucking the top two to three young leaves and throwing them into a basket on their backs, is done mainly by women who start work around 4am. The leaves are then transported to the factory where they are dried, chopped, fermented,

### RECOMMENDED TEAS

Black Label is top-quality tea, and Paul & Virginie is the strongest. For a novelty gift, pick up a packet of coconut-flavoured Le Dodo tea, made by Bois Cheri Tea Company. Other flavours include vanilla, lemon and passion fruit.

Signs will direct you to tea tastings

Tea from the Bois Cheri estate

self-guided informative exhibition on tea and the old machinery, and an interesting tour around the factory before a tea-tasting at a former hunting lodge. This is DIY tea bags with baby scones (on request) – but worth it for the panoramic view of the south.

A traditional Mauritian set lunch is served at the elegant Le Saint Aubin, 12km (7½ miles) south and five minutes' drive from the pounding sea at Gris Gris. A sugar plantation house set in tropical gardens, owned by the same family, it was built in 1819. If tea has led to a taste for something stronger, like a Vaco cocktail with vanilla rum and coconut, there's a guided tour around the tiny rum distillery here – the only place on the island to produce agricultural rum – and a chance to learn about vanilla production.

*To book, tel: 626 1513/1730. Factory: Open: daily (summer); Wed (winter). www.larouteduthe.mu*

cleaned and sifted in preparation for storing, sorting, blending and packing.

**La Route du Thé** (the Tea Route) is an excursion offered by the Bois Cheri Tea Estate, which has produced tea for over 100 years. As the organised tour includes a tasting and lunch, it's the best way to do it.

The four- to five-hour route kicks off at Domaine des Aubineaux in Curepipe, the elegant colonial home of the estate's owner which was built in 1872. The house has been left as it was when the family lived here, with furniture from all over the world and an extensive display of photographs. The road then winds across Plaine Champagne for 15km (9 miles) before dipping into the cheery Bois Cheri Tea Factory and museum, which has a

### VANILLA AS VIAGRA

Vanilla is a member of the orchid family, and of 100 types only three are cultivated. Vanilla Bourbon is cultivated in Mauritius and takes nine months to reach maturity. It's a popular flavouring here – found in everything from tea through cocktails to desserts. Vanilla is also a natural aphrodisiac, which is why it's also used for candles and mood-setting perfume.

## THE SOUTHEAST

All visitors to Mauritius arrive in the southeast, as this is where the airport is situated. However, the area is surprisingly untouristy and, unless staying around here, few visitors return. Romantic ruins, monuments, sites of historic battles and museums make the southeast a fascinating trip through Mauritius' colonial history. This part of the island has a feel of the old Mauritius in the villages and unspoilt coastal scenery, and it remains untouched by mass tourism. It is home to ecotourism parks and reserves, the largest animal park and a wilder, less visited coast, although not during the annual Pirogue Regatta. The southeast also hosts Mauritius' only Marine Park, Blue Bay, one of the top spots for snorkelling, and the only offshore nature reserve, Ile aux Aigrettes, thought to have been the last home of the mysterious dodo.

### Blue Bay

The closest public beach to Mahébourg, Blue Bay has the most stunning underwater scenery close to shore on the island. The Blue Bay Marine Park is a protected area and, for that reason, visitors are encouraged to go on glass-bottom boat trips, or organised snorkelling excursions to preserve it. But if you can, launch yourself from the coastguard's office and snorkel over some breathtaking coral.
*Glass-bottom boat trips travel over the Marine Park from the jetty, although they vary in quality. Recommended operators include Totof (Tel: 637 6342. Email: boatotof@yahoo.com) and Tam Tam Travel & Tours (Tel: 631 8642). Call first to avoid rogue operators. See also box opposite.*

### Gris Gris

Excursions on this coast always include a stop at Gris Gris, a dramatic clifftop overlooking a rough sea that gives a taste of the wilder side of Mauritius. The waves pound basalt rocks in front of a powder sand beach on this, the island's southernmost point. Steps lead down to the beach, and at very low tide it's possible to peek into caves under the cliff. Take a walk along the clifftop (*see p74*) to really get away from it all. *Most people stop off on an excursion, but you can take public transport, taxi or hire car.*

### Ile aux Aigrettes

A coral outcrop, surrounded by a limpid sea, about 1km ($2/3$ mile) off the coast of Mahébourg, Ile aux Aigrettes (Egret Island) is the nearest visitors can get to the Mauritius of 400 years ago. This 25ha (62-acre) island, established as a nature reserve in 1985, may have been home to the last dodo, now remembered in bronze at the entrance, and has some of Mauritius' last remaining coastal forest with ebony, orchids and rare palms. Managed by the Mauritius Wildlife Foundation (MWF), it has become an international standard for the

## EXCURSIONS FROM BLUE BAY

Several operators organise excursions from Blue Bay, mostly starting from Pointe Jerome near the Preskil Hotel. Tam Tam Travel & Tours offers day trips with Croisières Turquoises catamaran to Ile aux Cerfs up the coast, as well as two-hour boat trips out to Ile aux Aigrettes. Joceyln and his daughter at Totof provide off-the-beaten track small-group day trips on a purpose-built trimaran to the islands off the southeast coast – Ile de la Passe, Island aux Fous and Ile Vacoas. This includes plenty of snorkelling opportunities and a barbecue lunch on one of the islands.

*Totof. Tel: 637 6342. Email: boatotof@yahoo.com.*

*Tam Tam Travel & Tours. Tel: 631 8642. Call in advance to book. Excursion fee.*

protection of natural resources and endangered species. Giant Aldabra tortoises lumber under the 7m (23ft) high canopy, and endemic geckos and lizards live here. The trail here passes 20 endemic plants, with the rare Telfair skink in an enclosure. Ile aux Aigrettes is a breeding ground for the Pink pigeon, where it lives in the semi-wild.

*Tel: 631 2396. www.ile-aux-aigrettes.com. Departures for guided tours (1½ hours): Sat 9.30am, 10.30am & 1pm, Sun 9.30am & 10am; otherwise, it's a 5-minute boat ride from just below the Preskil Hotel, Blue Bay. Book tours in advance. Admission charge.*

Glass-bottomed boats at Blue Bay

## Robert Edward Hart Memorial Museum

Robert Edward Hart is Mauritius' most famous poet, awarded the Legion of Honour by France. Although he wrote in French, he was of British-Irish descent. If going down to Gris Gris, it's worth popping into this small museum in what was once his home, where his poems and personal objects are displayed.

*Le Nef, Souillac. Follow the signs through the residential streets; it's close to Gris Gris. Tel: 625 6101. Open: 9am–4pm. Closed: Tue. Free admission.*

### WORD OF WARNING

Rochester Falls, 5km (3 miles) from Souillac, are the prettiest on the island, but it is unwise to visit them independently. Local residents have been known to demand money for jumping into the falls, and turn ugly when tourists refuse to pay. Some taxis refuse to go there.

## La Vanille Réserve des Mascareignes

It was Charles Darwin who sent Aldabra tortoises here from the Seychelles to save them from extinction, and La Vanille, set up in 1985, is currently the only place in the world to breed them. They range in size

The creatures at La Vanille come in all shapes...

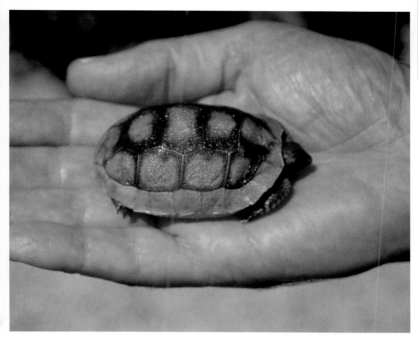

... and sizes!

from tiny hatchlings to Domino, who is over 90. This is a great place for young families as there are donkey rides and a jungle adventure playground. Around 500 tortoises live among the lush tropical foliage, although the main fascination may be with the thousands of Nile crocodiles (made into handbags and belts in the gift shop and served as fritters, kebabs and curry in the Hungry Crocodile restaurant). It takes two to three hours to look around this extended animal park with deer, cheeky Macaque monkeys, wild boar and even an Insectarium, with one of the world's largest collections.

*Senneville, 2km (1¼ miles) south of Rivière des Anguilles. Tel: 626 2503. www.lavanille-reserve.com. Open: 9.30am–5pm. Admission charge. Most people take an excursion here, but it's possible to get a bus to nearby, take a taxi or drive by hire car as it's well signed from various places.*

## EXCURSION: KAYAKING UP THE GRANDE RIVIÈRE SUD-EST

At 34km (21 miles), Grande Rivière Sud-Est (Southeast), marking the boundary between Flacq and Grand Port districts, is the longest river in Mauritius. Catamarans or boats usually take visitors on it, but you could kayak the 20 minutes to a lovely waterfall with Carlie Ltee (*www.ecovoyages.net*).

# Diving

Almost entirely surrounded by a barrier reef, with the overhangs and caves characteristic of a volcanic island, and clear warm waters and a good variety of marine life, Mauritius has some of the best dive sites in the Indian Ocean. From diving in aquarium-like areas filled with tropical fish and witnessing big fish such as tuna, wahoo and marlin, to diving in canyons or swimming with sharks, Mauritius provides something for both novice and advanced divers and, importantly, has friendly, professional and relaxed operators.

Twenty-three dive centres are registered with the Mauritius Scuba Diving Association (MSDA) (*Tel: 454 0011. www.msda-cmas.org*). Many are based in hotels, although there are some independent operators,

Diving in Mauritius can be like swimming in a tropical aquarium!

mainly in Grand Baie. Diving is well regulated here, with most operators members of internationally recognised organisations such as the Professional Association of Diving Instructors (PADI), National Association of Underwater Instructors (NAUI) or Confédération Mondiale des Activités Subaquatiques (CMAS).

Three levels of diving are available on the island. Most centres offer beginner dives that lead to either an introductory certificate or an internationally accepted 1-star certificate. The second level is for qualified divers with an updated logbook who can join one of two dive times (*9.30am & 1.30pm*) operated by most of the dive centres, six days a week. Most of these dives are to a depth of 10–30m (33–98ft). The third level, for experienced divers only, is deep diving, down to 60m (197ft) as well as diving in less frequented areas. Specialised divers often head for the virgin sites in nearby Rodrigues (*see p109*). Take a recent medical certificate, and some operators may also want to see divers' logbooks. As experienced divers will know, make sure you allow 24 hours between diving and taking a flight.

Diving here is year round, although the best time is from October to December and March to April. Diving is also regional, with the greatest concentration and widest range of dive sites in the north, including rewarding diving around the northern offshore islands. Other regions that have diving or dive centres include the southwest, west, northwest, east and south. Dive centres tend to cover the dives in their own regions.

MUGS club at Vacoas

The most popular dive sites lie off the west coast, around Flic en Flac and Trou aux Biches. Wreck-diving adds a mystique and historic element to diving here.

## TOP FAVOURITE SITES
**Cathedral, Flic en Flac:** The island's top dive, this is a huge cave full of colourful tropical fish, and drops off to around 30m (100ft) at its deepest point.

**Aquarium, Trou aux Biches:** As its name suggests, this is a place to see a wide variety of corals and fish, some quite rare. It's a good site for beginners.

**Water Lily, Trou aux Biches:** This is a well-established site featuring three water barges sunk in 1980.

**Whale Rock, Grand Baie:** This is a suitable drift dive around submerged black slabs of rock. At its deepest point, it includes canyons and caves.

**Passe St Jacques, Le Morne:** Sightings of black-tip sharks are guaranteed on this drift dive.

## DIVE CENTRES
**North**
**Atlantis Diving School**
*Trou aux Biches. Tel: 265 7172.*

**West**
**Villas Caroline Dive Centre**
*Flic en Flac. Tel: 453 8450.*

**MSDA**
To find a dive centre near your resort, *tel: 454 0011. www.msda-cmas.org*

Qualified divers can chat to resident divers at Mauritius Underwater Group Survey's (MUGS') Tuesday-night BYO BBQ at its clubhouse in Phoenix. The only member of the British Subaqua Club in the southern Indian Ocean, MUGS founded diving in Mauritius and also rents out equipment.

# Drive: Curepipe to Gris Gris

*This full-day drive passes through some of the most varied and exciting scenery on the island, from the plains to the highest peak in the densely forested interior and along the wild southwest coast. (See 'Food and drink' to choose a restaurant with a view.)*

*The drive covers 73km (45 miles) and will take around 8 hours.*

*Passing the Curepipe Gardens, turn left following the sign to Grand Bassin, and left again at La Marie and head up to Plaine Champagne. After about 7km (4 miles), opposite the Petrin Information Centre turn left along the road signposted to Grand Bassin. A 33m (108ft) tall statue of Shiva signals the car park.*

## 1 Grand Bassin

An hour's walk on the circular path around this crater lake and Hindu pilgrimage site includes the Hanuman temple atop the hill.

*Return to the car park and retrace your route, and then turn left opposite the Petrin Information Centre. Turn right at the next small roundabout. After about 5km (3 miles) stop at a car park with signs to Black River Peak.*

## 2 Black River Peak viewpoint

Looking down the impressive Black River Gorges to the mountains beyond, to the left is the Black River Peak, at 828m (2,717ft) the highest point in Mauritius, with a lovely waterfall opposite.

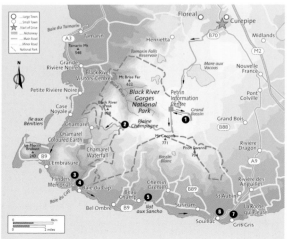

*Continue across Plaine Champagne and, coming out of the trees, wind down to Chamarel. Turn left to visit the Chamarel Coloured Earth, or continue straight on, turning left onto the B9 at Case Royale. After 4km (2½ miles), the bare rock face of Le Morne will loom to the right and about 10km (6 miles) later you'll arrive at Baie du Cap.*

### 3 Baie du Cap inlet

Perhaps the most stunning stretch of road on the island, the road winds beside the wild coast and by pretty untouched coves, into this steep inlet with rock overhangs and caves in the lush foliage.

*Just past the huge rock at the end of the bay that marks an ancient boundary, make a stop at the Flinders Memorial, on the right by the sea.*

### 4 Flinders Memorial

This bronze monument marks the unplanned six-year stay of the famous explorer Matthew Flinders. Arriving at Baie du Cap, he was arrested by the French as a spy.

*Continue along the B9 for about another 10km (6 miles), and look out for a rocky island on your right, close to the shore.*

### 5 Ilot aux Sancho

The first island taken by the British in 1810, before the historic battle of Grand Port. For a little adventure, wade out to this rocky outcrop and take the path under the trees to an anchor thought to be from a pirate ship.

*Continue another 7.5km (4½ miles) on the B9 to Souillac, passing the renovated old sugar mill at Bel Ombre. Turn right at the sign to the Social Security Office which brings you opposite the Robert Edward Hart Memorial Museum.*

### 6 Robert Edward Hart Memorial Museum, Souillac

Mauritius' most famous poet lived and wrote in his home here in the 1940s and 1950s. It's now a museum dedicated to his work.

*Facing the museum, turn left to arrive at Gris Gris car park.*

### 7 Gris Gris

A clifftop viewpoint over a wild sea that pounds onto basalt rocks by a beach below, Gris Gris is the place to taste the wild south coast.

*From Souillac, join the A9 for a speedier scenic route if returning to Curepipe.*

The dramatic coast road at Baie du Cap

## Domaine de Lagrave

Although not as beautiful as some, this small 202ha (500-acre) domaine is kept as close to its natural state as possible, and with no quad biking it is a good place to spot wildlife. Self-guided trekking is offered around Mount Lagrave, with trails divided into three levels of difficulty. The blue trail runs along the foothills for 3km (2 miles), the red trail up to the top for 6.5km (4 miles) and the black trail is a strenuous scramble up, rewarded with great views over Lion Mountain and the southeast coast. A three-course table d'hôte lunch is served in very simple surroundings on request. *Village Banane, Eau Bleu. Tel: 570 1849. www.parclagrave.com. Book in advance. Admission charge.*

## Domaine du Chasseur

Domaine du Chasseur was the first sugar estate to be turned into an eco-park. It's a place for walks through ebony, cinnamon, eucalyptus and Travellers palm. It's also the best place to see the Mauritius Kestrel, the island's only bird of prey, as almost half of the 550 birds live here, as well as Java deer, Macaque and wild boar. The Domaine offers quad biking, pistol shooting, snorkelling, deep-sea fishing and sailing by bamboo pirogue to the islands, as well as mountain trekking along 28km (17 miles) of track in its 1,500ha (3,707 acres) of 300-year-old subtropical forest. A trek to the top takes two hours and is rewarded with a 360-degree view of the island from the top. Bring insect repellent! The alfresco Panoramour Restaurant has one of the island's best lunchtime views – of the Bambous Mountains sloping into an aquamarine sea – and is often included in excursions. It also serves perhaps the most adventurous menu, with items such as roasted

The stunning view from the Panoramour Restaurant in Domaine du Chasseur

A Ylang Ylang tree at Domaine du Ylang Ylang

wild boar, duck and deer curry.
If you want to stay, seven romantic,
African-style eco-chalets are tucked
away on the property.
*Anse Jonchée. Well signed, it's about
3km (2 miles) up a private road just
past Vieux Grand Port. Tel: 634 5011.
www.dchasseur.com. Open:
8.30am–4.30pm. Admission charge.
Go by hire car, excursion or taxi.*

## Domaine du Ylang Ylang

Discover how perfume is made and
pick up essential oils at the Ylang Ylang
farm just below Domaine du Chasseur.
A jeep safari and restaurant are still
advertised on the billboard, but have
disappeared from the menu to leave
only a tiny distillery producing five
essential oils: Ylang Ylang, Lemongrass,
Eucalyptus, Camphor and Pink Pepper
can be bought in the shop along
with a range of Ylang Ylang products

from bath oil to candles (also found in
the Caudan Craft Market, *see p130*).
You can buy natural lemongrass insect
repellent here.

Although a brief description of the
process is given to visitors year round,
the most interesting time to go is
between October and April when the
Ylang Ylang tree flowers, and the
distillery is working.
*Anse Jonchée. Tel: 634 5702. Open:
9.30am–4/4.30pm. Free admission.*

### THE FLOWER OF FLOWERS

Ylang Ylang was originally brought to
Mauritius from the Philippines by Pierre
Poivre in 1750, and planted in
Pamplemousses (*see p42*). A yellow, long
flower with a delicate scent, called 'the flower
of flowers' by perfumers and mainly used as a
fixer for an aromatherapy oil, it's useful
against stress, anxiety and insomnia, high
blood pressure and tiredness.

## HISTORIC SOUTHEAST

*'The Lion Mountain dipping its toes in the bay of Mahébourg.'*

Malcolm de Chazal, Mauritian poet

### Mahébourg

Named after Mahé de Labourdonnais, 50 years after his death, Mahébourg was founded in 1804 by the French governor Charles Decaën, near the fort where the Dutch raised the first flag in 1598. It was once a busy port and a lively town with a racecourse during English rule. It is still characterful and, with fewer tourists than Port Louis, a place to taste the flavour of old

## BERTRAND FRANCOIS MAHÉ DE LABOURDONNAIS

Born at Saint Malo in 1699, little did Bertrand imagine when he joined the Royal Navy as a ship boy at the age of ten that he would go on to be appointed Governor of Ile de France (present-day Mauritius) by the East India Company. Mahé de Labourdonnais, as he is known, took over in 1734, moving the capital from Mahébourg to the more sheltered Port Louis. As soon as he set foot on the island, he started on an 11-year development and construction programme that provided the colony with a road network and developed its agriculture. Bertrand was architect, engineer and constructor of Port Louis, and also waged a systematic war against the maroons (deserting slaves) and traded slaves from Mozambique.

Pier at the Waterfront in Mahébourg

View across Grand Port Bay from Mahébourg

Mauritius. If possible, visit on a Monday when the market brings the town to life. However, on any day, you can watch the action from the terraces of a few rustic restaurants on the main drag.

## THE BATTLE OF GRAND PORT

The battle of Grand Port raged from 20 to 28 August 1810, and is a source of pride for the French – it was the only battle they won in the Napoleonic Wars, despite British trickery. The English and French captains, Willoughby and Duperré, both wounded, were nursed in what is now the National History Museum. Yet victory was short-lived. Having failed to take the island from the south, the British entered from Cap Malheureux at the island's most northerly tip, claiming the island as their own in December of the same year.

Mahébourg has several claims to importance, being built on the bay of Grand Port, the first place the Dutch landed and the site of Mauritius' most famous battle. Its National History Museum exhibits the bell from *Le San Géran*, which was shipwrecked in 1744 carrying the first sugar refinery machinery from France to the island, but was only discovered in 1966.

A recent addition to the city is a pink-paved promenade, the Waterfront, which makes a pleasant 1km (2/3 mile) stroll, where you can pick up some *gajaks* (snacks) at one of the stalls and eat them looking out to sea. There's a monument to French and English seamen lost in the battle of Grand Port at Pointe des Regates (Regatta Point), a breezy headland that overlooks the bay

In Bois des Amourettes (Young Lovers' Wood), in between the Ylang Ylang farm and Vieux Grand Port, French soldiers used to duel over girls they met here. Just off the coast are the caves of Salles d'Armes, where swords were also found, now only accessible by sea.

where it took place and has views over Ile aux Aigrettes and Ile de la Passe, which defended the main route into Mahébourg Bay. Named after its sphinx-like shape, the 480m (1,575ft) Lion Mountain forms the moody backdrop to the bay, and Dutch settlers are known to be buried at its foot.

### National History Museum

Housed in an elegant 18th-century colonial house at the end of a driveway surrounded by woodland, the National History Museum is worth a visit just for the grand entrance, let alone Mahé de Labourdonnais' bed, and the bell from the shipwreck of *Le San Géran* that inspired Mauritius' most famous legend (*see p15*), and always features in excursions to Mahébourg. It has rooms dedicated to the naval battle of 1810 and to the Dutch, French and British periods.

*Tel: 631 9329.*
*www.mauritiusmuseums.org. Open: 9am–4pm. Closed: Tue. Free admission. Bus, taxi or hire car on the main route into Mahébourg.*

### Rault Biscuit Factory

About 1km (²⁄₃ mile) north of Mahébourg, this family-run factory is on every tour of the southeast. A tour is more interesting than it sounds, as this family has been producing biscuits from manioc – a Creole root vegetable – by hand since 1870. It ends with a tasting of the biscuits imaginatively flavoured with custard, cinnamon, chocolate and coconut.

*Signed from Cavendish Bridge, north of Mahébourg. Tel: 631 9559. Open: Mon–Fri 9am–3pm. Closed: weekends. Admission charge.*

Lion Mountain viewed through the mangroves at Dutch Monument

### POINTE DU DIABLE (DEVIL'S POINT)

Odd compass readings experienced by ships passing this point are blamed on the devil that guards the treasure here. However, any possible pirate signs have long been removed as the French army moved here in the 1750s.

## Fort Frederik Hendrik

Vieux Grand Port is the oldest settlement in Mauritius, now a fishing village with pirogues bobbing in the sea. Blink and you'd probably miss it. Few historical remains are left, apart from Fort Frederik Hendrik in a garden sloping to the sea, well signed at the northern end of town. Here visitors can walk through the 17th-century ruins of the first Dutch fortifications, with a French layer on top, for commanding views across the bay. The Frederik Hendrik Museum in the grounds houses well-planned exhibits of what was excavated here.

**LOOKING FOR LUNCH?**

One of the few restaurants along this lonely coast, the rustic Le Barachois (*Anse Bambous, Vieux Grand Port. Tel: 634 5643. Email: le.barachois@yahoo.com. Open: 9am–5pm. Booking not necessary for lunch*), just before Devil's Point, specialises in prawns and crab farmed on the premises. It serves a great four-course lunch in a quiet spot beside the sea.

*Frederik Hendrik Museum, Vieux Grand Port. This is an isolated part of the coast, easier to reach by hire car than bus. Tel: 634 4319. Open: Mon–Sat 9am–4pm, Sun 9am–noon.*

The southeast

A private island in the bay of Grand Port

# Eco-adventures on Mauritius

A long list of eco-adventures is available on Mauritius, from climbing the mountains, visiting pristine islands off the coast, exploring an island nature reserve, through hiking in the national park to privately guided excursions by kayak or bike. However, the greening of Mauritius has been led by the opening of ecotourism playgrounds on vast private sugar estates, with near-native forest teeming with wildlife such as deer, monkeys and rare birds.

## NORTH

**❶ Domaine les Pailles, near Port Louis**

The Domaine most suitable for families, this 1,500ha (3,700-acre) nature park at the foot of the Moka Mountains offers mountain tours by 4x4, horse or quad bike, and train and horse-drawn carriage rides.

*Les Guibies, Pailles. Tel: 286 4225.*
*www.domainelespailles.net*

## WEST

**❷ Casela Yemen Nature Escapade, near Flic en Flac**

Yemen has guided half- and full-day hiking, double-quad, mountain biking and 4x4 rides in a 4,500ha (11,120-acre) African-style savannah where antelopes and zebra roam.

*Cascavelle. Tel: 452 0693.*
*www.caselayemen.mu*

## SOUTHWEST

**❸ Domaine L'Étoile, near Montagne Blanche**

Half-day quad, 4x4 trips, botanical and other treks and mountain biking are offered through the forested mountains of this 15,380ha (38,000-acre) estate.

*Tel: 433 1010 or 727 1050 (mobile).*
*www.cieletnature.com*

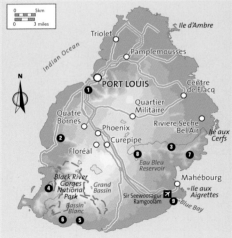

**4 Domaine Louisa, Chamarel**

Parc Adventure is an army-style obstacle course through a forest, across bridges and up climbing nets, open to children age six and upwards. *Tel: 234 5385/727 0869 (mobile). www.parc-aventure.com*

**5 Les Cerfs Volants, east of Bel Ombre**

The only zipline adventure park in the Indian Ocean, half-day courses run for 2km (1½ miles) over Rivière des Galets in the grounds of St Felix Sugar Estate. *Tel: 212 5016 or 422 3117/3120 (mobiles). www.lescerfsvolants.com*

**6 Valriche Nature Reserve, Domaine de Bel Ombre**

The newest nature reserve to open, this offers half-day quad and 4x4 adventures, trekking or day trip with trekking, and quads in a 1,012ha (2,500 acre) nature reserve with its own 150m (500ft) waterfall. *Tel: 623 5615/729 4498 (mobile). www.domainedebelombre.mu*

---

**GREEN MAP**

Pick up a copy of the *Mauritius Green Map* from Mauritius Tourism Promotion Authority (MTPA) offices around the island (*see p145*). It gives contact details of island-wide adventures ranging from sea-kayaking to climbing mountains.

---

**SOUTHEAST**

**7 Domaine du Chasseur, Anse Jonchée**

The first sugar estate to turn eco-park is still a favourite, offering quad biking, pistol shooting as well as mountain trekking in its 1,500ha (3,707 acres) of forest where the Mauritius Kestrel can be easily spotted. *Tel: 634 5011. www.domaineduchasseur.mu*

**8 Domaine de Lagrave**

Self-guided trekking on Mount Lagrave is provided on this 202ha (500-acre) nature park, with great views over Lion Mountain and the southeast coast from the top. *Village Banane, Eau Bleu. Tel: 570 1849. www.parclagrave.com*

**9 Beachcomber Sport & Nature**

Beachcomber is currently the only hotel group to offer an ecotourism programme to its guests. Activities include mountain biking, kayaking and abseiling. *Shandrani Hotel. Tel: 603 4540. www.beachcomber-hotels.com. Activities only available through Beachcomber hotels.*

# Drive: Phoenix to Devil's Point

*This largely historic drive goes from the centre of the island through a pretty nature reserve to the major historic sites along the fascinating southeast coast. Intersperse the history with the Ylang Ylang farm and/or a trip to Blue Bay. It's worth doing this drive on a Monday to catch Mahébourg's atmospheric market.*

*The drive covers a distance of 43km (27 miles) and takes around 6–8 hours.*

*From Phoenix, take the motorway south past the Phoenix Brewery, taking a left at junction 16, signed 'Midlands', just past Curepipe. In Midlands village, turn right to Eau Bleue and follow the road through Banane, until you see the signpost on the left to Le Val Nature Park, about 1km (²/₃ mile) before Cluny. Take the potholed track up through a gate (open: 6am–5pm) and down the hill. Tell the guardian you're going to Le Val.*

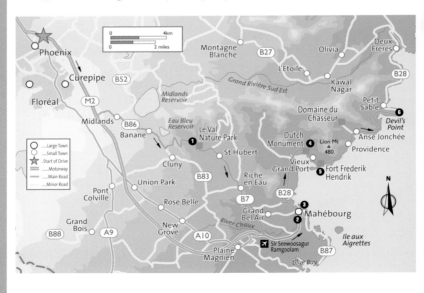

### 1 Le Val Nature Park

Unless it's lunchtime, there's not much to keep you at Le Val. Just pay the small admission charge for this scenic drive that offers lovely views over Lion Mountain and the southeast coast as you descend to the park.

*Continue through the reserve through St Hubert, and after 3km (2 miles) turn left past Riche en Eau sugar estate and drive through a pretty, quiet tree-lined road. Turn right at a roundabout towards the airport, and after 2km (1¼ miles) turn left to take the A10 to Mahébourg. Turn right if you want to take a side trip to Blue Bay. The National History Museum is on the left, as you enter Mahébourg.*

### 2 National History Museum

The injured commanders of the French and English fleets were treated in this grand French colonial house surrounded by woodland, after the battle of Grand Port in 1810. Now, among the cannons and memorabilia lies the bell of the *Le San Géran* that inspired Mauritius' most famous legend (*see pp15 & 96*).

*Continue into Mahébourg until you see the police station. Turn right after it, down Rue des Mariannes, and park at the Waterfront.*

### 3 The Waterfront

This paved promenade makes a pleasant 1km (²⁄₃ mile) stroll. Surrounded by *gajak* (snack) stalls, it has monuments to soldiers and slaves, and views over the bay where the famous battle of Grand Port took place.

*Continue driving through Mahébourg until just over the River Chaux, with its stories of pirate treasure, and turn right to Vieux Grand Port (no sign).*

### 4 Dutch Monument

This monument, to the right in the mangrove just below Lion Mountain, is where the Dutch first landed in 1598 and named the island Mauritius.

*Continue on the coast road past small fishing villages and Ferney Sugar Estate, and look out for the Fort Museum by the sea on your right after Vieux Grand Port.*

### 5 Fort Frederik Hendrik

First built by the Dutch in 1638, the fort ruins now seen by the edge of the sea are French (*see p97*). It had fallen into disrepair before the Battle of Grand Port.

*Continue on, taking a left turn to visit the Ylang Ylang farm or straight on to Devil's Point.*

### 6 Devil's Point

Built in the 1750s to protect Mahébourg Bay, the stonework defences here are among the finest 18th-century workmanship in Mauritius (*see p96*). The national monument on the hill gives lovely views over the bay.

# Deep-sea fishing

Mauritius is one of the best spots in the world for deep-sea fishing. The sea drops to 70m (230ft) just 1km (⅔ mile) from the coast, meaning that huge fish are there for the taking 15 minutes from shore. Its tropical waters are home to blue and black stripe marlin, sharks, tuna, sail fish, bonitos, wahoo, dorado and the *bécune* (barracuda). The island held the world fishing record for blue marlin for 15 years and holds several other fishing records including a 505kg (1,115lb) Mako shark, a 181kg (400lb) blue

shark, a white tuna that weighed in at 102kg (224lb), a bonito of 19kg (41½lb) and a barracuda of 57kg (125lb). African records mention a yellow tuna of 96kg (212lb) and a white tuna of 102kg (224lb). Recently caught blue marlin weighed in at 650kg (1,430lb) and 615kg (1,355lb).

The most popular season for international anglers is from September to March, but big-game fishing is possible year round, although it changes with the season (*see below*). Traditionally, caught fish remained the property of the boat owner, but a tag and release policy now operates from many hotels.

### WHEN TO FISH FOR WHAT

Year round – barracuda, black marlin, skipjack tuna
Mar–Apr/May – yellow fin tuna
Sept–Dec – hammerhead shark/wahoo
Nov–Mar/Apr – sailfish, blue marlin, Mako shark.

A half or full day's boat charter can be booked through most hotels, and a number of professional fishing companies can organise boat charters for a half or full day's deep-sea fishing. Vessels are modern and well

Make sure you have a record of your catch!

equipped with radio and trolling equipment and include a knowledgeable skipper. They typically have three fighting chairs on the stern, and outriggers to troll five baits at any time designed for a maximum of six anglers. Snacks and drinks are usually provided – some even offer a barbecue on board. Being tax-free, Mauritius is also a great place to buy fishing tackle – one of the best-known shops is Quay Stores in Port Louis.

Most hotels can organise a charter

With a huge blue marlin in the clubhouse, the historic Le Morne Anglers Club in Black River village (*Tel: 483 5801. www.morneanglers.com*) is the only internationally recognised fishing club on the island, and a member of the IGFA, but it's members only. This is where the prestigious Marlin World Cup is hosted every December, sponsored by La Pirogue resort (*www.marlinworldcup.com*). Sunset Holidays organises the Sunset Bill Fish Classic every February (*www.worldwidefishingsafaris.co.uk*).

Although fishing trips go out from the north and east too, it is at Flic en Flac on the west side that you can catch big fish. Here, the continental shelf drops to more than 600m (2,000ft) 1.6km (1 mile) from shore. Although in its infancy, Rodrigues Island now has a couple of companies offering deep-sea fishing charters.

**PROFESSIONAL DEEP-SEA FISHING CHARTER COMPANIES**

**NORTH**
**Sportfisher, Grand Baie**
*Tel: 263 6309.*
*Email: karen@intnet.mu*

**EAST**
**Surcouf**
*Tel: 419 3198.*

**WEST**
**West Sails Ltd, Black River**
*Tel: 483 5060/728 7979 (mobile).*
Has a contract with several hotels including La Pirogue.

**RODRIGUES**
**Rod Fishing Club**
*Tel: 875 0616.*
*www.rodfishingclub.com*

A full list can be found by area at *www.mauritiustourism.co.uk*

## EXCURSIONS

Taking an organised excursion is the most popular, convenient way to see the sights around the island and couldn't be easier – just hop on a minibus, and go. A wide variety of organised excursions is on offer from all major hotels by a small number of well-regulated providers (*see opposite*). These range from half-day shopping trips, helicopter tours, and eco-adventures on a 4x4 or quad bike, to undersea adventures or day trips by catamaran to pristine islands. Local providers, such as those who own glass-bottom boats at Blue Bay, also have their own excursions. In addition, a growing ecotourism offering includes privately guided tours, from forest walks and scaling mountains to getting active on a bike or kayak.

### Land excursions

These include themed tours across regions, but not going too far afield, such as 'shop til you drop', the 'Tea Route', the 'sugar adventure', and 'time gone by', which visits the colonial mansions. There are more elaborate themes such as 'adventure', usually visiting Domaine L'Étoile or Domaine du Chasseur, or 'nature and history', travelling from Mahébourg's National History Museum to the southeastern attractions of La Vanille Réserve des Mascareignes and out to Ile aux Aigrettes. There are also regional tours focusing on attractions in a region such as the scenic south, with options to, say, shop, or, alternatively, combine this with a visit to Casela Bird Park in the west. Some excursion operators, such as MTTB-Mautourco, offer more half-day options for those who have less time; for instance, bargain hunting inland at Quatre Bornes market and adventure at Valriche Nature Reserve in the southwest, as well as a full day at one attraction, such as Domaine du Chasseur, for those who would

Take a catamaran cruise to Tamarin Bay to see dolphins

You get a different sort of view on an underwater adventure

like to savour rather than have a taste of Mauritius.

## Sea excursions

Mainly by catamaran, these tend to be day-long excursions and include a barbecue lunch on board and time for snorkelling. They classically head east to the Grande Rivière Sud-Est and its waterfall before stopping at the island playground of Ile aux Cerfs, west into Tamarin Bay to see the dolphins, or to the Northern Islands or on an underwater adventure. A popular full-day excursion also goes to Ile aux Cerfs. Some, such as MTTB-Mautourco, offer a sunset catamaran cruise.

## Ecotourism excursions

These are privately guided, often tailor-made excursions, and tend to be geared towards active people, although many are suitable for families. Land excursions include mountain biking in private reserves in the north and

southwest, mountain climbing all around the island, and trekking, mainly in Black River Gorges National Park, as well as the more extreme sports of canyoning and abseiling. Sea excursions include sea-kayaking around some of the lesser-known islands (*see Directory for providers*).

## Main excursion operators
**MTTB-Mautourco**
84 Gustave Colin Street, Forest Side.
*Tel: 670 4301. www.mttb.com*

**Mauritours**
Rue S Venkatesananda, BP 125, Rose Hill.
*Tel: 467 9700. www.mauritours.net*

**White Sand Tours**
M1 Motorway, Cassis, Port Louis.
*Tel: 212 3712. www.whitesandtours.com*

**Summertimes**
5 Avenue Bernardin de St Pierre, Quatre Bornes.
*Tel: 427 1111. www.summer-times.com*

**Connections Tourism Management Ltd**
Crater Lane, Floréal.
*Tel: 696 9933.*
*Email: connect-resa@intnet.mu*

---

### TAXI!

Looking for a reliable taxi for a personal excursion? Try Dave (*D&D Rapid Service. Tel: 750 0108*), who worked for an excursion company for 20 years. He is knowledgeable and speaks excellent English.

# Getting away from it all

*Although Mauritius is one of the most densely populated islands on earth, getting away from it all is easier than you might imagine. Inland in the southwest, the Black River Gorges National Park has a large swathe of forested hills criss-crossed with hiking trails, or why not climb a volcanic peak (see p72) or visit a Domaine or ecotourism park (see pp98–9)? Out to sea, there are excursions to the paradise islands you've dreamed of (see opposite & p108), and driving or walking in the south leads to a wild, untamed coast. Then there's Rodrigues Island, part of Mauritius, but a 90-minute flight away.*

You can go mountain-biking at La Nicolière

## ISLAND LIFE
### North
### Kayaking around Ile d'Ambre (Amber Island)

Patrick Haberland's Yemaya Adventures, named after the African goddess of the sea, offers sea-kayaking expeditions around the little-visited Ile d'Ambre. Expeditions are typically for a full day, and include optional snorkelling in the mangrove, a guided hike to the old ruins and a lunch stop at the nearby tiny island, Pointe Bernache. Modern double or single kayaks imported from South Africa are used, and the trips are tailor-made according to level and interest, and are all personally escorted. Suitable for children of eight years and upwards. *Yemaya Adventures based at Grand Gaube. Tel: 752 0046. www.yemayaadventures.com. Adventures offered daily for a fee. Book in advance. Clients need to get themselves to the start point.*

### Southwest
### Ile aux Bénitiers (Clam Island)

Crescent-shaped Clam Island, known to the locals as 'Coco Island' because it's covered in coconut trees, lies in the lagoon off La Gaulette village near Le Morne and can be visited on a day trip by catamaran or kayak. Only 2km (1¼ miles) long and 0.5km (⅓ mile) wide, this tiny island has clear white beaches, without much sharp coral. It's very private and not too deep, so great for swimming. *Croisières Avasion, Beau Bassin. Tel: 728*

**AMBER ISLAND**

Named after the ambergris once found there, Amber Island is important both ecologically and historically. Surrounded by mangrove, an important breeding ground for fish, it is also where the *Le San Géran* was shipwrecked on 17 August 1744, giving birth to Mauritius' most famous book and legend, *Paul et Virginie* (*see p15*).

*1574 (mobile). Depart: 9.30am, on island for 1½ hours, barbecue on board, back by 4pm.*
*Dolswim. Tel: 258 9821.*
*http://dolswim.intnet.mu. Depart: from Island Sports Hotel, Black River 8am or 10am, for full day, swimming with dolphins in Tamarin, and a swim at Ile aux Bénitiers.*
*Kayaking: Yemaya Adventures. Tel: 752 0046. www.yemayaadventures.com. Excursions charge and lunch included in above tours. It's not recommended to take an ordinary boat from the beach.*

A Yemaya Adventures expedition around Amber Island

## Southeast
### Iles des Deux Cocos
### (Island of the Two Coconuts)

Visitors are met at the jetty with cold, perfumed towels and sparkling wine. As you sink into luxurious white sofas in an open-sided tent next to a thatched bar serving tempting homemade rums, it's not difficult to believe in paradise. Offered exclusively by Naiade Resorts, this island excursion has all the luxury trappings that you'd expect, without the gimmicks. Small and not far from shore, with powder-white beaches, it's idyllic and interesting – visitors can go on a glass-bottom boat or snorkel over the stunning reef of the Blue Bay Marine National Park nearby. Lunch is a highlight, with an excellent high-quality, plentiful buffet and faultless service. A tour around the Folly reveals a sumptuous Moroccan-style villa retreat with a bath, big enough for four, filled with rose petals. The Folly was built in 1925 by the British governor

Sir Hesketh Bell to entertain his mistresses. Rumours of treasure led him to dig here and, suspiciously, he left for England soon after.
*Bookings: Tel: 423 1752.*
*Email: individual.CRO@naiade.com or through Naiade hotels, which includes speedboat transport.*
*If individually booked, pick-up is from the jetty off the Blue Bay road (next to Coastguard station). Excursion from 10am until around 4pm.*
*Excursion charge.*

## ON LAND
## North
### Cycling at La Nicolière

Ex-cycling champion Patrick Haberland runs unique mountain-biking trips around the 30km (18½ miles) of track in the private reserve of La Nicolière on the central plain. The reserve has a good variety of scenery, and Patrick knowledgeably points out wildlife such as wild pigs, stags, birds and bats, and

Rodrigues Island is a short hop in a plane

A deserted beach on Rodrigues Island

the various endemic and indigenous plants. There's a view over the Northern Islands, before dipping down among the raffia plants to La Nicolière reservoir. All adventures are personally led and can be tailor-made, but typically range from a half day and gentle to challenging, depending on skill. Children aged 12 and over are welcome.

*Yemaya Adventures, Grand Gaube. Tel: 752 0046. www.yemayaadventures.com. Excursions daily; book in advance. Excursion charge. Clients need to get to the start point.*

## Rodrigues Island

Referred to as the anti-stress island, Rodrigues is a sleepy, rustic island with a laid-back charm. Here, women in straw hats spear octopus in the clear lagoon and fishermen still set sail in traditional wooden pirogues. Just 17.5km (11 miles) long and 8km (5 miles) wide, with a lagoon double its size, it's a place to go for relaxation and simplicity. With few cars in sight, Rodrigues offers Creole culture, large doses of fresh air, organic chicken and octopus, and around 20 secluded beaches.

Key places to visit include its capital, Port Mathurin, just seven streets wide; Trou d'Argent, 'The Money Hole', a wild cove where pirates once landed; Caverne Patate, where an hour's tour takes in stalagmites and stalactites; Ile aux Cocos (Coconut Island), a white, sandy, bird sanctuary where noddies bob in the wind while visitors laze in the shallows; and the Giant Tortoise Project which opened in 2007.

Walking trails crisscross the island, and it has a reputation as a good place for diving (there are three dive centres around the island; closed July and August), deep-sea fishing (marlin, skipjack tuna and sun fish; best October to April) and kitesurfing (best May to September, based at the Marouk Hotel).

*Air Mauritius offers flights to Rodrigues, four times a day in peak season. www.airmauritius.com. Demand is high, so book well ahead.*

Pick up 'A Guide to Rodrigues' from Mauritius Tourism Promotion Authority (MTPA) offices and check out their useful website *www.rodrigues-island.org*. A good range of adventure tours and activities is offered by Ecotourisme Rodrigues Ltd (*Douglas Street, Port Mathurin. Tel: 831 2801. Email: ecotours@intnet.mu*).

# When to go

*When planning activities, bear in mind that Mauritius has a microclimate, which means that it could be raining where you are with the sun shining a few kilometres away, or vice versa!*

The island lies 20 degrees south of the equator, just above the tropic of Capricorn in the warm Indian Ocean, and has a tropical maritime climate. Although known primarily as a winter sun destination, with opposite seasons to Europe, Mauritius is generally sunny and pleasant on the coast throughout the year. The heat here never rises to uncomfortable levels, but sometimes it can get a little sticky and oppressive at night. May to October, the island's winter, is warm and dry. Summer, from November to April, is hot, humid and rainy. During the height of the rainy season, from January to March, cyclones may strike the island, or pass nearby, meaning heavy rainfall and sometimes violent winds. The sea breeze blows steadily from the southeast all year round. July and August can see strong winds on the south and east coasts, which in summer transform into a welcome cooling breeze.

Average temperatures range from 17°C to 24°C (63–75°F) in August to between 23°C and 33°C (73–91°F) in January, and the water temperature is between 22°C and 27°C (72–81°F). The west and north are warmer and have less rain than the east and south. Average rainfall varies from around 900mm (35in) on the coast to 1,500mm (59in) inland. Curepipe has the highest rainfall of the inland towns, and it rains on Plaine Champagne at

Sun and stormy skies near Le Val Nature Reserve

Choppy waves crash against the Pont Naturel on the southwest coast

any time of year. Humidity is 75–85 per cent year round.

December to January is peak season in Mauritius and best avoided. There's a big mark-up on holiday prices in December and also at Easter. Discounted holiday packages are more likely outside of French school holidays, and October and November are perhaps the best time to travel, when the price is right and the weather is good. Some people find the peak of summer by the northern coast unbearably hot.

## When to do what

November to April is the best time of the year for diving as waters are clear, calm and warm; June to July is the worst time. Divers and other water-sports enthusiasts should avoid the peak cyclone season in January and February. June to August is best for surfing. The best deep-sea fishing (*see p102*) is from October to April – the blue marlin season. Hikers, cyclists and climbers may prefer the cooler, drier months from June to September when there aren't as many mosquitoes at large. Interest can be a strong factor in planning a visit. If you're into horse racing, for example, the season runs from November to May, and if you want to catch one of the spectacular festivals, check the dates (*see p18*).

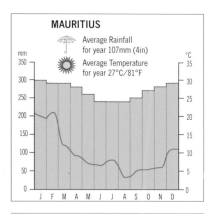

**MAURITIUS**

Average Rainfall for year 107mm (4in)

Average Temperature for year 27°C/81°F

**WEATHER CONVERSION CHART**

25.4mm = 1 inch

°F = 1.8 × °C + 32

# Getting around

*Mauritius has one major highway, which snakes up the country from the airport in the southeast to the main tourist centre of Grand Baie in the north. Although the island is small, the generally narrow roads mean that driving anywhere takes time. However, sightseeing is easy when all you need to do is board a minibus for a half- or full-day excursion, hire a car or taxi or, perhaps, travel by local bus for the experience.*

### Excursions

Reasonably priced and with a selection of half- and full-day tours to all the main sites. With most large operators, the fee includes lunch and entrance (*see p104 for details of operators and routes*).

### Helicopter tours

Four-seater Bell Jet Ranger Helicopters, operated by Air Mauritius, offer tours lasting from 15 minutes to an hour, giving a stunning bird's-eye view of the island. They also have flights to the

You'll find public transport in the strangest places, including banana groves!

most beautiful golf courses, or an hour's flight and drop-off for two hours for lunch somewhere special. Book through your tour operator, hotel or directly (*Tel: 603 3754. Email helicopter@airmauritius.com*).

## Taxis

Tourist taxis are regulated and linked to hotels or provinces – this information printed in a yellow panel on the driver's door. They're relatively inexpensive, with the cost of journey varying depending on where you're staying and how long you're going to be. Hiring a taxi for a day is usually a cost-effective option. Tipping isn't expected, but is appreciated.

## Public transport

A cheap and reasonably efficient bus service runs to every corner of the island, apart from the uninhabited parts of Plaine Champagne and Grand Bassin. As the service is informal, you can be dropped off outside most of the tourist sites mentioned in this guide. Buses are particularly useful if you are

---

### TAXI TIPS

Although taxis have meters, fares can be negotiated for a return journey, and a cheaper rate is usually found away from the hotels. Taxis are used to taking tourists to the usual places, but not all drivers, even at hotels, speak English well. If you want to do anything unusual, buy a good map (*see p145*) to guide the drivers around. Also be aware that if you stop at the shops they suggest, most drivers are on commission.

---

doing a one-way walk and don't want the expense of taxi pick-up and drop-off. However, you'll need time, and outside of peak times you will probably need to change bus for a trip of a few hours or more. Try and pick a full bus because empty buses often trawl around the backstreets at about 3km an hour, honking and looking for customers. Tickets are purchased from an on-board conductor.

Government bus companies ply different parts of the island. The main three are the National Transport Co (NBC) (*Tel: 426 2938*), United Bus Services (UBS) (*Tel: 212 2026*) and Mauritius Bus Transport (MTB) (*Tel: 245 2539*). Regional operators are Triolet Bus Service (TBS) (*Tel: 261 6516*) and Rose Hill Transport (RHT) (*Tel: 464 1221*). In addition, private, government-regulated operators serve the island, their buses emblazoned with names as preposterous as 'Good Luck', 'Magical Mystery Tour' and 'Bad Boys'. Buses operate from 5.30am–8pm in built-up areas, from 6.30am–6.30pm in the countryside. A bus passes the many simple bus stops throughout the island every 20 minutes. *Info Guide* (Editions Le Fleuron, 2006), sold in bookshops on the island, is full of town street maps and has excellent bus route maps, useful for independent travellers.

## Hiring a vehicle

Driving is on the left here, and it's compulsory to wear a seatbelt. Roads are often narrow, with no pavements and plenty of people and dogs. Although improving in tourist areas, towns and attractions are poorly signposted, and when usually calm, considerate and even-tempered Mauritians get behind the wheel, they can transform into impatient and erratic drivers.

Driving in Mauritius isn't for the faint-hearted, but hiring a car is still a popular, flexible and inexpensive way to tour the island. A valid driver's licence is required, and drivers must be over 23 years old. Speed limits are 80km/h (50mph) on the motorway and 50km/h (30mph) in built-up areas. Petrol is cheap, and all of the international retailers are represented here but tend to be expensive.

Car hire companies Hertz (*Tel: 670 4301. Email: hertz@mautourco.com*) and Avis (*Tel: 208 6031. www.avismauritius.com*) have all the latest models, including trendy open-topped jeeps and four-wheel drives. If cost is a consideration and you're happy with something basic, try one of the local providers such as ADA (*Tel: 675 2626/251 4234. www.ada.fr*), which will work out 30–40 per cent cheaper. All the above have offices at the airport. Motorbike hire is available from Grand Baie, organised through Grand Baie Travel & Tours (GBTT) (*Trou aux Biches. Tel: 265 5261. www.gbtt.com*).

## Domestic flights

Air Mauritius (*Tel: 207 7575. www.airmauritius.com*) has the most frequent flights to Rodrigues, an 80-minute hop away, four times a day in peak season. Book well in advance.

Sir Seewoosagur Ramgoolam International Airport (SSR), or Plaisance Airport as it is known, is approximately 3km (2 miles) from Mahébourg, 48km (30 miles) from Port Louis, 70km (43½ miles) from Grand Baie, 45km (28 miles) from Flic en Flac and 40km (25 miles) from Belle Mare. It takes from 10 to 90 minutes to drive to hotels from the airport, with an average travel time of 40 minutes. For a speedier arrival at your hotel, take a helicopter transfer.

Take care when driving, you may encounter an overloaded sugar cane lorry like this

Taking a domestic flight will give you great views of Mauritius' beautiful landscape

# Accommodation

*Mauritius has a higher density of 5-star hotels than anywhere else in the world. Think colonial-style resorts with personal butlers, personal plunge pools and arrival by helicopter, or luxurious villas. Accommodation here tends to be on the expensive side, but some excellent mid-range and simple family-run hotels can be found in most areas. Moreover, an increasing number of hotels offer good-value all-inclusive packages. Other options include private* campements *or 'weekend houses' to rent islandwide, apartments, villas, and beach bungalows called* pieds dans l'eau *(feet in the water) by the locals. There are also* chambres d'hôtes *(bed and breakfasts), some at very competitive prices.*

There are no campsites on the island. A few interesting options exist in the interior, such as staying in old colonial mansions or lodges, almost all associated with a Domaine or eco-tourism offering. The most recently developed area, where four new secluded hotels opened at the end of 2004, is Bel Ombre in the untamed southwest. Mauritius' first boutique hotel, Hôtel 20° Sud (*see p150*), opened near Grand Baie in 2005.

## Hotels

Five main hotel groups operate here: Beachcomber, Kerzner International – One&Only Resorts, Naiade Resorts, Constance Hotels and Veranda Resorts. The well-known international chains such as Hilton, Oberoi, Sofitel, Méridien and Taj can also be found. What distinguishes Mauritian hotels is

their high level of service. Even in 3- or 4-star hotels, the service is better than on other tropical islands and is certainly the best in the Indian Ocean. Over 100 hotels and resorts are dotted around the island, nearly all overlooking the island's white sand

### STAY IN A HOT NEW HOTEL

The 5-star Shanti Ananda spa resort (*www.glahotels.com*) opened on the south coast in December 2006. With 55 suites and villas fronting the beach and set in a spacious 14ha (35 acres) of tropical gardens, this is the place to go for seclusion. Heavenly spa treatments are available in one of 17 treatment rooms. A second Club Med (*www.clubmed.co.uk*) opens on the island in 2007 in Albion Village, aimed at child-free couples, or those with older children. The first Four Seasons (*www.fourseasons.com*) will join the glamour on the east coast in 2007, with a 119-room hotel with two outdoor pools, a kids' club, spa, 18-hole golf course, and more.

beaches, and offering the ingredients of a holiday from heaven, from kids' clubs to golf, and from spa treatments to every water sport imaginable.

## Self-catering

Self-catering accommodation is mostly concentrated in tourist areas with facilities such as Grand Baie, north of Belle Mare in the east, and in the west around Flic en Flac. However, there are options islandwide if you know where to look. They range from basic concrete blocks at a bargain price to exclusive villas with a butler and prices to match. Once only found through word of mouth, they now advertise and accept bookings over the internet.

## Villa or beach bungalows

Villas de Maitre (*www.villasdemaitre.com*) has a good selection of villas and beach bungalows around the island, as does Elegant Destinations (*www.elegantdestinations.co.uk*). An

The main pool at Le Touessrok resort, Trou d'Eau Douce

array of tempting apartments can be found at *www.mauritius-islander.com* and Mauritius Individuell (*www.mauritius-individuell.com*).

Typical offerings by small outfits include Seapoint Beach Bungalows (*Tel: 696 4804. www.seapointbungalows.com*) with studios, apartments and beach bungalows at Pointe aux Canonniers, Grand Baie; the budget studios and apartments offered by Pingouinvillas (*Tel: 637 3051. www.pingouinvillas.com*) near Blue Bay; cheap, clean and cheerful art deco apartments offered by Résidence Art (*Tel: 453 5277*) on Royal Road, Flic en Flac; and Les Lataniers Bleus (*Tel: 483 6541. http://leslataniersbleus.com*) with three villas around a swimming pool next to the beach in Black River

village. Le Preskil Beach Resort has reasonably priced, private rustic lodges made out of stone and thatch, Les Lodges d'Union, inland from the south coast and Andréa, in a pretty spot at Rivière des Anguilles, near Gris Gris (*Tel: 604 1000. www.lepreskil.com*).

You can stay in a colonial-style house, such as this one in Le Saint Aubin

A room at La Barachois in Vieux Grand Port

A renovated private villa on a peninsula can be found with Yemaya Shores (*www.yemayashores.com*), the kind of place usually only found by word of mouth. Les Chalets Verangue (*Coeur Bois, near Le Morne. Tel: 483 6610*), attached to Le Verangue sur Morne restaurant, is an unusual choice, nestled privately in the forest below Plaine Champagne.

## DO YOUR RESEARCH

Each region of the island has a slightly different vibe and landscape, offers varied activities, and lies near different attractions, so it's worth considering what you want from your Mauritian holiday before booking accommodation. If you're mainly interested in water sports, it would make sense to stay near Grand Baie or the east coast. If you have small children, the west coast has some of the safest beaches. For nightlife, head to Grand Baie in the north, but for tranquillity, try Le Morne in the quieter southeast, or southwest at Bel Ombre. Mauritius is small, but bear in mind that it takes time to travel between regions when choosing accommodation.

## SPECIAL INTERESTS

Want to know if there's a kids' club, kitesurfing or spa at a hotel? Try the search facility on the Mauritius Tourism Promotion Authority (MTPA) website (*www.mauritiustourism.co.uk*). At the time of writing, 13 hotels had spas, about the same had facilities for the disabled and 30 offered deep-sea fishing trips.

# A taste of Mauritius

Eating in Mauritius is a great pleasure as the cuisine is as interesting as it is varied, with a collision of world culinary traditions that has created something unique. The island's hotels serve plenty of exotic seafood dishes, including *camarons* (freshwater crayfish), giant prawns and freshly harvested oysters. Venison and wild boar have made it onto menus from French hunting traditions on the island, and palm hearts or 'millionaires salads' are often served with smoked blue marlin, another speciality here. The Creole influence is rich in tomatoes, onions, ginger, garlic and chillies, such as in *rougailles* (an African spicy tomato paste). Other traditional dishes include *daube* (beef or chicken stew), *vindaye* (deep-fried fish coated in turmeric, ginger, chillies and mustard seeds), *snoeck rougaille* (salted fish in traditional tomato sauce), *kalya* (meat or fish cooked with saffron and garlic or ginger), and the use of *chevrettes* (freshwater shrimp) and *tec-tec* (clams).

There's plenty of fresh fruit grown on the island, with *litchis* (lychees), mangoes, pineapples, papaya and

Chillies drying in the sun – a much-used ingredient in Mauritius

A *gajak* seller in Mahébourg

on town streets, markets or even in backyards all over the island, selling mainly Indian specialities including *dholl purri* (a soft, savoury pancake stuffed with mashed split peas and *rougaille*), *roti* (pancakes filled with meat and potato curry) and *samosas* (deep-fried pastry pockets stuffed with curried vegetables). Vans sometimes specialise in one dish such as *gateaux piments* (deep-fried chilli and split pea cakes). The street vendors in larger towns such as Port Louis, Curepipe, Quatre Bornes and Grand Baie often offer the traditional Creole accompaniments, *rougaille* or *achard* (shredded carrots, cabbage, beans and cauliflower cooked al dente with garlic and onions). Port Louis has the highest concentration of street vendors selling Chinese noodles and broths, and in Chinatown you'll find glass cases full of Chinese cakes. The Muslim's contribution to Mauritian cuisine is *briani* or *halim* (a thick soup of mutton, lentils and rice) as well as halal kebabs. Hawkers in towns and often beside public beaches at weekends serve these, some open late into the evening. Stalls sell pineapple peeled and carved into a spiral, which makes a refreshing snack. Fresh King Coconut juice can be found in towns, at tourist attractions and beside public beaches alongside Western fast food.

bananas found on street stalls or in the island's markets, and definitely on your breakfast table. Mauritians don't typically eat out much, but they munch on *gajaks* (snacks) all day and buy lunch out. To find local specialities, leave your hotel and take your cue from the office workers – follow them to food stalls and sit in the park, or go to one of the scruffy-looking but popular eateries.

## Street food

It's easy and usually safe to try street food in Mauritius – mostly of an Indian and African flavour with a dash of French. You'll find carts or bicycles, with a glass case on the back, parked

# Food and drink

*The cuisine in Mauritius reflects the diversity of its multicultural people, whose ancestors came from countries with strong culinary traditions – France, India and China. These cuisines coexist with something uniquely Mauritian when mixed with the Creole influence. Eating in Mauritius is exciting – where else could you eat fresh baguettes for breakfast and octopus vindaloo for dinner? The Chinese eat curry, Indians have fried rice and, traditionally, Franco-Mauritians have rice and Creole specialities at midday, and a European-style dinner.*

## Dining out

Dining out can be as casual or glitzy as you wish. Fabulous value-for-money Chinese, French and Indian restaurants are dotted around every town, although Grand Baie has the highest concentration, along with international restaurants such as Japanese and Italian. Lunch can be savoured with table d'hôte Creole specialities in a rustic atmosphere in Chamarel in the southwest. Alternatively, enjoy lunch or dinner in an elegant setting at one of the Domaines, with lovely locations on the old sugar plantations around the island, serving mainly Creole classics with a French twist. At hotels, there's everything from dining à la carte by candlelight beside the beach to casual beach barbecues. For a really special evening meal, Mauritius' 5-star hotels are home to top restaurants, including Le Gavroche des Tropiques at the Voile d'Or, overseen by celebrity chef Michel Roux Jnr who uses the cinnamon, vanilla and limes grown on the island to flavour dishes. Spoon des Iles at One&Only Le Saint Géran is the first Alan Ducasse restaurant to set up outside France.

Fish-eaters will have a ball here, with plenty of seafood to choose from. However, vegetarians may find it difficult to find a staple protein as cheese and eggs don't abound outside hotels, but there are plenty of vegetable curries, bean dishes, varied salads and fresh fruit at hand.

If you don't want a full meal, pick up a cooked-to-order snack at a stall

A much-repeated anecdote is about a businessman on the island who liked to start the day with a full English breakfast, have an Indian curry for lunch and finish with a Chinese meal in the evening. That's Mauritius!

Phoenix, the famous beer of Mauritius

Food and drink

## Local tipples

The local tipple is rum, made from the sugar cane grown across the island – Green Island Rum is the most famous and often mixed with fruit juice to create delicious rum cocktails. Perhaps more interesting though are the agricultural rums made from the first pressing of the sugar cane on some Domaines, as well as in homes, often combined with the vanilla grown here, or steeped with local fruit.

Mauritius produces some award-winning and therefore very drinkable beers. Phoenix, the oldest and main brewery on the island, produces two lagers: Phoenix, referred to in Creole as 'spider beer' because the label looks like one, and the slightly stronger, at 6 per

Bringing in the sugar cane, source of local rum

cent, Blue Marlin. Otherwise, there's the higher-proof Black Eagle lager, produced by a newer, Indian brewery. It may surprise you to discover that Mauritius also makes its own wines, the Oxenham range, although the grape is imported. Try Eureka or, if you want to go more upmarket, something bearing the St Nicholas label. Whisky is the preferred Mauritian tipple, but it is expensive here.

Local soft drinks to try include tamarind juice and *alooda*, a sweet milky drink with black falooda seeds that swell up like sago, flavoured with rose syrup and sweet basil.

## Tipping

Many restaurants include a service charge, but the waiting staff still expect a tip. Most people leave some change or up to 10 per cent of the bill. Cafés and pubs in more touristy areas also expect a tip, but it's not compulsory to give one.

# Entertainment

*Mauritius is not the place for a raucous holiday. As the hotels are mainly on the coast or isolated inland, away from the towns, entertainment tends to be hotel-based. The larger resorts offer everything from cabaret shows and discos to intimate dining, soft piano bars and weekly Sega dancing performances.*

There are some excellent restaurants in the Caudan Waterfront that are attractively lit up at night. Other than this, the liveliest nightlife is found at Flic en Flac and Grand Baie on a Friday and Saturday night. Flic en Flac is inexpensive, but it's really only Grand Baie that is buzzing in the evening. Grand Baie has a variety of nightlife, from trendy bars to the widest range of international restaurants and several nightclubs. Nightclubs often charge a small entrance fee, although women sometimes get in free.

Mauritius is also not a place to get cultural. It's too far from anywhere to attract more than the occasional international artist or performer. The main cinema, with three screens and showing English-language films, is at the Caudan Waterfront in Port Louis. There are also cinemas in Rose Hill, Curepipe and Mahébourg, although the films tend to be dubbed into French. There are two theatres on the island, one in Port Louis and one in Rose Hill.

### COCKTAIL HEAVEN

Two hotel bars renowned across the island for their cocktails are the Maritim, particularly lively on a Friday night – just ask for their 'Special' – and the Prince Maurice, which has designed their own, 'The Splendour of the Prince', served at the Laguna Bar overlooking the lagoon.

'What's on' listings can be found in newspapers, but may be in Creole, French or English. There are casinos in

A cold beer, Ruisseau Creole shopping centre, Black River

Curepipe, Domaine les Pailles and Port Louis that attract a mix of locals and tourists to the slot machines and tables. Open in the early evening, the tables open at 9pm Monday to Saturday and 3pm on Sundays. They are also found in Trou aux Biches, One&Only Le Saint Géran, La Pirogue and Berjaya Le Morne hotels.

As for daytime entertainment, there are a few good museums, but it tends to centre on shopping centres, some of which sport art galleries, and French-style cafés frequented by both tourists and locals. Local culture is best experienced in the street life of markets, snack stalls and annual religious festivals.

Mauritians don't tend to dine out in restaurants much in the evening, eating their main meal at home. Instead, they congregate around snack stalls on public beaches on Saturday nights, the men with their guitars poised ready for some Sega. Other than that, you may be lucky and catch an Indian wedding, when the whole extended family gathers to celebrate, with traditional food eaten from banana leaves, using the fingers.

Places to meet both locals and ex-pats are Rotary Clubs in the main towns and Lions Clubs in Port Louis, Quatre Bornes and Curepipe. Golfing guests are able to visit the inexpensive bar and restaurant at the Gymkhana Club, where Thursday night is darts night. Experienced divers can obtain temporary membership of the

Dine at an elegant restaurant such as Clos Saint Louis, Domaine les Pailles

Mauritius Underwater Group Survey (MUGS) club and join their clubhouse BYO BBQ on Tuesday nights. Anyone can join a friendly crowd of expats and locals at the Hash House Harriers, the 'drinking club with a running problem', which meets every second Sunday morning in off-the-beaten-track spots around the island (*www.mhash.com*). A nominal fee includes a run, drinks and lunch.

# Honeymoons on Mauritius

Mauritius is one of the world's top five hotspots for honeymoons and weddings. Couples have an incredible choice of over 100 mainly 5- and 4-star resorts hugging the coast, most overlooking the island's white-sand beaches. Then there are the top-quality spas, gourmet cuisine, tropical climate and excellent service. Unlike other tropical island destinations, there's a lot to see and do here, from hiking around impressive volcanic peaks in the interior to diving on the coral reef circling the island. Honeymoon packages may include gifts, flowers and fruit, dinner, or a spa treatment.

An idyllic wedding on a romantic island

**FIVE HOTELS MADE FOR HONEYMOONERS**

**Dinarobin Hotel Golf & Spa**

Between the dramatic Le Morne Mountain and a white-sand beach, this 172-suite hotel is in one of the best spots on the island. It has a stunning infinity pool, sumptuous Clarins Spa with saunas, Turkish baths, Jacuzzi and an 18-hole golf course.
*www.beachcomber-hotels.com*

**Hilton Mauritius Resort & Spa**

A big resort, this suits couples who don't want to hide away, and who like activities – think horse-riding, mountain biking and free water sports. The 193 rooms are sea-facing, light and airy, and there are four restaurants and nightly entertainment.
*www.mauritius.hilton.com*

**Oberoi Mauritius**

This stunning 5-star deluxe hotel with 73 rooms, 23 villas and 48 pavilions is by Turtle Bay on the northwest coast. The unusual architecture, amazing swimming pool, wonderful service and tasteful Eastern-inspired décor are complemented by Mauritian sugar-cane thatch roofs, volcanic boulders and tropical plants. A honeymoon

highlight is a private sunset catamaran cruise.
*www.oberoihotels.com*

### The Residence
An elegant plantation-style resort, afternoon tea is served on the veranda under elegant ceiling fans. The 163 rooms and suites are tastefully decorated with four-poster beds and cool tiled floors, and have views over a white-sand beach and turquoise lagoon. Private butlers, three restaurants and the Sanctuary Spa make it a haven.
*www.theresidence.com*

### Taj Exotica Resort & Spa
This hotel's 57 luxury villas are so exquisite that you'll feel like a celebrity. Each is private with its own plunge pool. Inside is a giant bed, polished wood floors and exquisite furnishings. The bathrooms are the most romantic on the island. The little extras, 24-hour butler service and mouth-watering Mediterranean cuisine on a candlelit jetty, all add up to extreme pampering.
*www.tajhotels.com*

### DREAM WEDDINGS
Civil and religious weddings in Mauritius are recognised in the UK. For civil weddings, couples need to visit the Registrar's office 24 hours in advance, but for religious weddings

Honeymoon in style at La Paradise

couples must be on the island for 15 days before the ceremony – time to work on that tan.

Most hotels have a coordinator to organise a tailor-made dream wedding. If you don't fancy a beach wedding, you could arrive by helicopter or get married underwater with Blue Safari Submarine (*see p38*). Hotels offer special wedding packages and, unlike some countries, weddings here are limited to one a day.

### FOOTBALLERS' PARADISE
Check into the Presidential Villa at La Paradise if you want to follow in the footsteps of former Manchester United star Roy Keane, or the Royal Suite at Le Touessrok where former England goalkeeper David Seaman honeymooned.

# Shopping

*Mauritius is one of the largest textile exporters in the world, supplying clothes for major international chains and designer labels. Holiday bargains include cashmere and traditional arts and crafts in the shopping arcades; sunglasses and jewellery in duty-free shops; and Indian bedspreads, spices, leatherwork and colourful baskets in the markets. Like other activities on Mauritius, shopping is a multicultural experience. Pretty French-designed sundresses coexist with African sculptures and drums, colourful Indian saris and religious art. The jewellery-making techniques brought by Indian and Arabian immigrants are still used, and the making of model ships evolved out of the melting pot.*

## What to buy

High-street brands and designer clothing exported to Europe originate in Mauritius, and seconds can be picked up in factory shops around the island. High-quality cotton, silk and linen clothes are found for bargain prices in shopping centres. Children's clothing is available through a number of retailers – Gecko Kids, Pomme d'Api and Tara

Duty-free jewellery shopping at Caudan Waterfront

offer a wide selection of garments for newborns to teenagers. Quality knitwear is a good buy here – cashmere, a speciality, costs a third of the price in the West. Mauritius is also known for handmade tailored suits, delivered within 24–72 hours (try *New Bombay Trading. Rose Hill. Tel: 464 0948*). For interesting designs, try Shibani which has an outlet at the Floréal Knitwear Shop in Floréal (*Tel: 696 9049*), said to be one of the best places to buy cashmere sweaters in the centre of the island. It also has shops in the Caudan, Grand Baie and Flic en Flac.

Perfume, jewellery and electrical goods can be purchased for discount prices in duty-free shops. Bright straw bags made here, *pareos* (sarongs), cotton T-shirts and imported Indian embroidered cushion covers are also good, inexpensive buys. Model ships are a unique local craft. Then there's the souvenirs – local rum and vanilla tea, spices, smoked marlin, anthurium flowers (the red flowers with yellow middles often seen in hotel decorations) and Sega CDs. And, of course, a miniature dodo.

## Duty-free shops

The sign 'Duty Free' appears on many shops, but in the official outlets there's a certain procedure. The main shops with this facility are jewellers, such as Adamas duty-free diamond boutique for fine-cut gems, Shiv jewels, designer clothes shops, electronics shops and, for handmade items, Ravior and Charles Lee. The tax rebate on these goods is around 40 per cent, but Hazara, the carpet dealers who pack and send purchases by air freight, take 100–108 per cent of the tax off.

There are two ways to buy duty-free goods. Either way requires payment in foreign currency, and showing your passport and ongoing/return air ticket. Traditionally, the tax is taken off goods and they're delivered to the airport to collect on departure. If you'd rather take your goods away with you, and you are shopping less than 48 hours before departure, if you pay the full price at the time of purchase you can claim a rebate (in the same currency) at the airport.

Mauritius will be a tax-free shopping haven by 2010, which means more bargains to be had. Plans are to take 80 per cent of tax off almost 2,000

Bags for sale at an arts and crafts market in Port Louis

goods, including clothes, textiles, jewellery and electronics. There will also be new shopping centres built around the island.

## Arts and crafts

**Glass Blowing** At the Mauritius Glass Gallery in Phoenix, watch artisans blow recycled glass into objects as varied as lamps, vases and dodos. Buy direct from the workshop or from shops at the Caudan Craft Market or Super U, Grand Baie.
*Mauritius Glass Gallery, Pont Fer, Phoenix. Tel: 696 3360. Email: mgg@intent.mu. Open: 8am–5pm. Free admission.*

**Model Ships** Around 40 years ago, Jose Ramar made a model ship for fun. Someone from the first French Embassy saw it and took it to France. There was much demand there for models, and the Embassy helped with the plans for famous ships such as the *Victory*, *Bounty* and *Le San Géran*. Mauritius has since built a reputation for the art and craft of building miniature copies of famous ships, with about 60 models to choose from. Built to the scale of the original plan, with every detail perfectly reproduced, the ships are made of teak or mahogany, with the sails usually dipped in tea to give them that ancient look. Although shops will send your purchase, or pack it well to carry on or put in the hold, airlines may charge for carriage according to size and weight.

Workshops around the island are open to visitors and ships can be bought on site:

**Comajora Ship Model Museum**
La Brasserie. *Tel: 670 0301. Email: comajora@intent.mu. Closed: Mon.*

**Historic Marine Factory**
Goodlands. *Tel: 283 9304. www.historicmarine.com*

**First Fleet Reproduction**
Phoenix. *Tel: 698 0161. www.firstfleetreproductions.com*

Indian textiles on sale in Flic en Flac

## Where to buy

Shopping excursions from hotels usually include factory outlets, duty-free shops and tourist shopping arcades, and typically focus on Grand Baie, Port Louis and sometimes Curepipe. For a more local and personalised experience, hire a taxi to take you around.

### North
### Port Louis

If you can only make one shopping trip, it should be to the capital, Port Louis. Here, air-conditioned malls at the Caudan Waterfront lie opposite the sprawling Central Market, factory outlets rub shoulders with small boutiques selling Indian saris, and street sellers line the cracked pavements selling everything from chickens to cheap Western clothing.

### Caudan Waterfront

The best loved of shopping centres in Mauritius, 'The Caudan', as it's affectionately known, is the island's most glamorous shopping centre. It has 60 shops, including branches of all the well-known outlets and duty-free shops. Probably the greatest attraction

Mahébourg market

is the range of gifts from paintings to spices in its traditional arts and crafts market, where crafts such as basket-weaving can be seen. The Caudan doubles as a leisure centre with art galleries, a museum, bars, restaurants, a three-screen cinema, and even a casino housed in a replica of a pirate ship. *Old Pavillon Street, Le Caudan. Tel: 211 6560 for the information kiosk. www.caudan.com. Open: Mon–Sat 9.30am–5.30pm. Late-night shopping Thur until 8pm.*

### Central Market
At the craft market upstairs, squeeze through alleys of sparkly sequinned shoes and gypsy skirts, pashminas, Indian bags, cushion-covers and bedspreads, *pareos* (sarongs) and fake designer T-shirts. There's a good selection of gifts, but bargain hard. *Between Queen and Farquhar streets. Open: Mon–Fri 6am–6pm, Sat 6am–noon.*

### Grand Baie
Grand Baie's Sunset Boulevard on Royal Road is an extensive open-air arcade, right next to the shore. Full of upmarket jewellery, crafts and clothing

**BE ON YOUR GUARD**

Watch out for taxis who try to take you to shops where they get commission. This is a common scam in Mauritius – and you end up paying for it.

boutiques, it is a good place for *pareos* (sarongs) and designer surfwear, at great prices. It has some unusual shops such as Vaco Art Gallery (*Dodo Square. Tel: 263 3106*), hung with colourful and tropical paintings by Vaco Baissac, one of the island's best-known artists.

### Central Mauritius
Factory outlets selling goods such as Ralph Lauren and Levis seconds at discount prices are found mainly in the inland towns, where 30 per cent of the population lives. If you have time to poke around, the little Chinese and Indian shops, and the shopping arcades in Rose Hill, Quatre Bornes and Curepipe are the places to find similar goods at half the price of tourist shopping centres. Try the well-established Sunnassee Arcade in Rose Hill, the Orchard Centre in Quatre Bournes, Currimgee, Salafa (good for jeans) and Yanpalach in Curepipe.

### Islandwide
Tourist shopping centres, such as Diane and Garden Village in Curepipe, are springing up around the island. Ruisseau Creole (*Tel: 483 800. www.ruisseaucreole.com*) is a good one on the main road between Tamarin and Black River.

# Sport and leisure

*Just about everyone in Mauritius is mad about English football. If you want to strike up a conversation with a local lad, try talking Man United or Liverpool. He'll probably be wearing one of the shirts to give you a clue. You'll find this national sport played everywhere from stadiums to scruffy patches of dirt between the filao trees.*

## SPECTATOR SPORTS
### Horse racing

Weekends between May and November see both tourists and locals form crowds of up to 30,000 to watch international jockeys at Champ de Mars racecourse in Port Louis. The Mauritius Derby is the main event on the calendar, held at the end of August. Check details on *www.mauritiusturfclub.com*

Many visitors tackle the hike to Le Pouce from Port Louis

## PARTICIPATION SPORTS
### Cross-country running

The Royal Raid A cross-country marathon started in Mauritius in 2006 and is scheduled to become an annual event, taking international runners 35km (22 miles) across the island every April (*http://runraid.free.fr* – *in French*).

### Cycling

Bicycles can be hired for just an hour or up to a day from major hotels and from some agencies in the north. Some hotels, particularly in the quieter southwest, offer cycle trails, but most cycling is done as a guided tour. The best cycling experience is to get out into nature, with Beachcomber through their hotels or, better still, with specialist Yemaya Adventures (*see p151*).

### Golf

A choice of seven 18-hole golf courses and five 9-hole courses on the island makes Mauritius a serious golfing destination. With courses set among the world's most beautiful hotels with stunning scenery to match, it's an inspiring place for a game. Most courses are in upmarket hotels, used by residents for no charge, but with a green fee for non-residents. Many hotels require non-residents to book tee-off times, and most offer professional instruction. The most celebrated are in the east and southwest of the island, although there are clubs in every region. The Bernard Langer-designed 18-hole golf course on Ile aux Cerfs must be one of the world's greatest golf settings, and you can even arrive by helicopter.

### Hiking/trekking

Most hiking trails in Mauritius lie in the Black River Gorges National Park on Plaine Champagne, where hikes vary from half an hour to a full day, and from easy to strenuous. Hiking is also offered on private land in the Domaines, which have opened up as ecotourism parks (*see p98*) and on Mauritius' mountains (*see p72*). The most popular mountain hike is up the thumb-shaped Le Pouce (*see p44*), suitable for the whole family. Others, such as Le Morne or Lion Mountain, are technical in parts and should not be undertaken without a guide.

### Horse-riding

Horse-riding is best done in the morning or late afternoon to avoid the heat of the day. Many hotels can arrange horse-riding, with stables scattered along the coast, although standards and safety vary considerably. Excursions are offered by the few professional stables on the island.

### Water sports

Mauritius is a mecca for water-sports enthusiasts. It offers waterskiing, sailing, windsurfing, kitesurfing, sea-kayaking and parasailing as well as first-class diving and snorkelling around the island. Plastic or sailing shoes should be worn as a precaution against getting cut on sharp coral, or stepping on stonefish, depending on what activity you're doing.

### Big-game fishing

*See p102.*

### Diving

*See p88.*

### Kayaking

The two places for sea-kayaking in Mauritius are up the Grande Rivière Sud-Est (Southeast) on the east coast to see a waterfall, and half- or full-day trips around the more isolated Ile d'Ambre (Amber Island) in the north (*see p107*), in addition to offerings by hotels.

### Parasailing

This is the newest craze to hit the island and soars up to 200m (650ft) from Grand Baie.

### Pirogue Regatta

This is a three-day race in the historic southeast during the second week of December. Either be in it, combining a stay with eco-activities in Mauritius, or be a spectator. For more information, *tel: 212 5016 or 422 3117/3120 (mobiles). www.lescerfsvolants.com*

### Sailing

The calm waters of the lagoon make Mauritius a good spot for sailing, and its epicentre is Grand Baie. Small dinghies are available at the large beach hotels or, if you want to go further afield, charter a yacht from the Grand Baie Yacht Club (*Tel: 263 8568.*

Try the latest activity, parasailing

Le Morne is one of the best locations for windsurfing and kitesurfing

*www.gbyc.info – in French*). Catamaran cruises are popular, and excursions are organised through many hotels. These excursions are usually a full day including lunch and snorkelling. The most popular cruises are to the Northern Islands or to see dolphins in Tamarin Bay.

## Snorkelling

The coral gardens of Mauritius are some of the best in the Indian Ocean, and opportunities for snorkelling abound all around the island. Snorkelling gear is usually complimentary from hotels, or it can be rented from dive centres or picked up cheaply from stalls and supermarkets in tourist areas. The best underwater scenery for snorkellers is found at Blue Bay Marine Park, Le Morne, Flic en Flac on the west coast, and Trou aux Biches and Turtle Bay marine park in the north.

## Waterskiing

The lagoons of Mauritius make great waterskiing spots. This is offered free of charge in more upmarket hotels and for a fee at many mid-range establishments.

## Windsurfing and kitesurfing

Mauritius has long been a favourite for windsurfers, particularly the windier east coast. It's now attracting the attention of kitesurfers, with Le Morne appearing on promotional ads as one of the best places in the world. There are five main kitesurfing schools here, all IKO (International Kitesurfing Organisation; *www.kitesurfing.org*) certified. Kitesurfing outfits are also found in Cap Malheureux and Grand Gaube in the north, and at Pointe d'Esny and Belle Mare in the east. Spots and schools can be found at *www.mauritiusurf.com*

# Spas

Mauritius can now provide a holiday for mind, body and soul in its top-quality spas, boasting a wide range of treatments and therapies from all over the world. Most hotels and resorts have luxurious spas with everything from Ayurvedic treatments based on India and Creole remedies sourced from local herbs and flowers to ocean-inspired treatments and exclusive products from top beauty brands and fashion houses such as Clarins, Givenchy and Shiseido.

The island's leading spas are at One&Only Le Saint Géran, Paradise Cove, Legends, The Royal Palm, The Hilton, Le Prince Maurice, Beau Rivage, The Oberoi, The Residence, Belle Mare Plage, Dinarobin, Voile d'Or, Heritage Golf & Spa Resort, Le Telfair Golf & Spa Resort and The Indian Resort. Some of these are open to non-residents, although you should book ahead.

## FIVE TOP-CLASS SPA PICKS

### Givenchy at One&Only Le Saint Géran

One of the few Givenchy spas in the world, this is found at Mauritius' most famous hotel. Choose from peels, wraps, jets, stones and electrotherapy to help with weight loss, body and skin conditioning, or try the four hands (two therapists) Ylang Ylang massage for a trip to paradise.
*www.oneandonlyresorts.com*

### The Jiva Grande Spa, Taj Exotica Resort & Spa

A small, private retreat for spa buffs and romantics who want to hang out in the private Jacuzzis of the couples' suites. Try one of the signature Indian treatments, such as Samattva, a massage to balance energies and release tensions, or an Ayurvedic consultation.
*www.tajhotels.com*

Lap pool at the Givenchy spa, Le Saint Géran

Relax with a drink and be pampered in a top-quality Mauritian spa

lag or an Oriental Beauty Treatment at Legends, built and furnished around the ancient Eastern principles of Feng Shui.
*www.naiade.com*

There is also a number of well-run independent spas around the island, suitable for those on a budget.

## TOP FOUR INDEPENDENT SPAS

### The Sanctuary, The Residence

This nine-room spa with soft cream furnishings offers treatments from exclusive Swiss cosmetic brand La Prairie. Try the WellSun treatment that combines steam bath, gentle exfoliation with sand and essential oils and a gentle massage, to prepare your skin for tanning.
*www.theresidence.com*

### Six Senses Spa, Le Telfair Golf & Spa Resort

Tranquil ponds and tropical gardens encircle the six indoor rooms and two outdoor gazebos at the only six senses spa in Mauritius. With its blend of ancient and modern treatments, it's one for serious spa goers.
*www.letelfair.com*

### Source at Legends

Pick from a range of thalassotherapy treatments, Hot Stone therapy for jet

### Gym Hydro Spa, Grand Baie

Offers massages, hammam and sauna.
*Tel: 263 4891.*
*www.grandbaiegym.com. Open: 9am–8pm.*

### Life Care Spa, Flic en Flac

Specialises in Japanese massages and mud baths.
*Tel: 453 9999.*

### Spa Viva, Quatre Bornes

This spa's vibrogym and Thai massage treatment are a great antidote to stress.
*Tel: 467 8907. Email: spaviva@intnet.mu*

### Surya, Pereybere

Specialises in Ayurvedic treatments from practitioners from Kerala in India.
*Tel: 263 1637. www.spasurya.com. Open: 9am–8pm.*

# Children

*Mauritians love children and you'll find a warm welcome all over the island, from hotel restaurants to the local markets. The beach is likely to be the main attraction for children here. As the lagoon is largely protected by the coral reef, many of the beaches fronting hotels have long clear shallows and gentle seas that are ideal even for toddlers, and as hotels have a plethora of water sports, teens will be equally happy in or on the water. The most family-friendly beaches are found at Flic en Flac, Belle Mare, Pereybère and Blue Bay. In addition, there are no poisonous snakes or insects on the island. In fact, the biggest danger you'll encounter in Mauritius is the strength of the sun. Pack plenty of sunscreen and a child-friendly mosquito spray.*

## Kids' clubs

Hotels on the island are becoming increasingly family-friendly with many organising kids' clubs. Most offer a mix of activities ranging from cooking to nature walks, painting to water sports,

Kids will love the safe beaches

as well as supervised trips to the beach and often their own pool and kitchen. Some have teen clubs that have lessons in water sports and a games room.

The following hotels (*see Directory*) all offer kids' clubs and babysitting for an additional fee:

### North

Maritim's Turtle Club (ages 3–11)
Le Victoria's Bob Marlin Mini Club (ages 3–12)
Legend's Little Mermaid Club (ages 3–11) and Teens Club (ages 12+)
Le Méridien's Penguin Children's Club (ages 4–12)
Trou aux Biches' Bob Marlin Mini Club (ages 3–12)
Le Mauricia's Bob Marlin Mini Club (ages 3–12)

### West

La Pirogue's Fun Club (ages 4–12) and Teens Club (ages 12–20)

**Southwest**

Indian Resort's Akuna Matata Club (ages 3–12) and Teens Club (ages 12–20)

Dinarobin's Bob Marlin Mini Club (ages 3–12)

**East**

One&Only Le Touessrok's KidsOnly (ages 4–12) and ClubOne (ages 12–18)

Beau Rivage's Little Mermaid's Club (ages 3–11) and Teens Club (ages 12+)

**Southeast**

Shandrani's Bob Marlin Mini Club (ages 3–12)

Le Preskil's Kids Club (ages 3–12). *Tel: 604 1000. www.lepreskil.com*

## Great family days out in five regions
**North**

L'Aventure du Sucre (*Beau Plan, Pamplemousses. Tel: 243 0660. www.aventuredusucre.com*) is an interesting interactive experience for ten-year-olds and upwards; Domaine les Pailles (*Les Guibies, Pailles. Tel: 286 4225. www.domainelespailles.net*) offers activities for all ages, from horse and carriage rides to quad biking, 4x4 and trekking, with an Italian restaurant for lunch overlooking a swimming pool that children can use. A northern attraction especially designed for families is the Mauritius Aquarium (*Tel: 261 4561. www.mauritiusaquarium. com*), with a touch pool, at Pointe aux Piments.

**West**

A catamaran cruise from Tamarin to see dolphins (*Croisieres Australes. Tel:*

*263 1669. Email: cruise@c-australes. com*), Casela Bird Park (*Tel: 452 0693. www.caselayemen.mu*) and African animals zoo for the little ones, and quad biking in nearby Yemen (*as for Casela above*) for teenagers – fun for all the family.

**Southwest**

Parc Adventure at Chamarel (*Tel: 234 5385/727 0869 (mobile). www.parc-aventure.com*) offers an army-style obstacle course. Nearby, at Valriche Nature Reserve (*Tel: 623 5615/729 4498 (mobile). www.domainedebelombre.mu*), there is a safari by 4x4 or quad bike – for teenagers and young-at-heart adults.

**East**

The Dolphinarium is the island's newest family attraction. Ile aux Cerfs has plenty of water sports for teenagers, a pirate boat for youngsters, and a chance to relax in the shallows and a gourmet lunch for parents.

**Southeast**

La Vanille Réserve des Mascareignes (*Tel: 626 2503. www.lavanille-reserve.com*) has donkey and tortoise rides for toddlers, crocodiles and monkeys to keep the older ones amused, and lunch at The Hungry Crocodile for all the family.

### TRAVELLING WITH CHILDREN

Flights from the UK are generally overnight, which makes a journey to Mauritius easier to manage with children.

# Essentials

## Arriving in Mauritius

### By air

The only international airport in
Mauritius is Sir Seewoosagur
Ramgoolam International Airport
(SSR), or Plaisance Airport, as it's also
known (*Code MRU. Tel: 603 3030*), in
the southeast of the island. There are
only two charter flights to the island,
Corsaires from France and LTU from
Germany.

**Air France** *www.airfrance.com*
**British Airways** *www.ba.com*
**Emirates** *www.emirates.com*
**Virgin Atlantic** *www.virgin-atlantic.com*

**Air Mauritius** (*www.airmauritius.com*)
is the main Mauritian carrier, offering
direct flights from Paris and London,
and over 25 flights a week from several
European cities as well as Australia
(Perth/Melbourne/Sydney) and South
Africa (Johannesburg, Durban and
Cape Town). There are no direct flights
from the USA, Canada or New Zealand,
but going via Asia – Air Mauritius flies
direct from Singapore, Malaysia, India,
Hong Kong – may offer good deals.
Most people coming from the USA or
Canada tend to fly via Paris or London.

Flight paths mean that Mauritius can
be combined as a twin-centre holiday
with glitzy Dubai, a safari in South
Africa, Kenya or Botswana, or as a
honeymoon following a wedding in the
Seychelles.

As an island, there are no options
to travel here by rail or road. Very
few people arrive by sea, unless on a
cruise liner.

Pick up a map to help direct you to some picturesque routes

## Customs

Visitors aged over 18 can import duty free:

200 cigarettes or 250g of tobacco
1 litre spirits, 2 litres of wine
250ml of eau de toilette, 100ml of perfume.

There is no limit on importing foreign currency, but there is a low limit on the export of Mauritian rupees.

## Departing

Airport departure tax is usually included in the price of your air ticket, rather than payable on departure.

## Electricity

Mauritius uses 220 volts AC for its supply. Most modern buildings and hotels, which usually have adaptors you can borrow, have three-pin plugs, and budget hotels the two round-pinned variety.

## Internet and email

As Mauritius strives to become a cyber island, most hotels have high-speed internet access and some offer in-room connection with a laptop. There are internet kiosks in many post offices accessed by a pre-paid card bought at the counter or by credit card. Internet cafés are usually found in the shopping arcades of main towns across the island. The select few listed below are open from 10am–5pm, and many close later, although not on Sundays.

Signs will keep you on the right road

**North**

**Zenith Cybercafé**

*Astrolabe Building, Port Louis Waterfront. Tel: 208 2213.*

**Cyber Pirate**

*Espace Ocean Building, Grand Baie. Tel: 263 1757.*

**Centre**

**Cyber2000**

*Centre Commerciale, Phoenix Sivananda Street. Tel: 698 5473.*

**West**

**Pasanda Internet Café**

*Spa Supermarket, Flic en Flac. Tel: 453 5631.*

**Southeast**

**Cybersurf Internet Exchange**

*Rue Labourdonnais, Mahébourg. Tel: 631 4247.*

## Maps

The Mauritius Tourism Promotion Authority (MTPA) produces a reasonable *Map of Port Louis & Mauritius*, marked with tourist sites. For something clearer, more detailed and current, but still small enough to be manageable, pick up the *Tourist Map* of *Mauritius & Rodrigues* published by editions Le Pritemps Ltee, a bookshop in Vacoas. Perhaps the most easily found up-to-date map is *Carte Touristique Ile Maurice* produced by Institute Geographique National (IGN) (*www.ign.fr*). Although more unwieldy, this Ordnance Survey map gives relief and road details.

## Media

There's a weekly English-language newspaper, *News on Sunday*, in Mauritius. TV channels run by Mauritius Broadcasting Company (MBC) have local news bulletins in English at 7am and 9pm, but Mauritius College of the Air (MCA) television tends to have more English programmes. Most hotels and resorts have satellite TV, including the news on Sky, CNN and BBC World.

## Money
### Currency

The currency used here is the Mauritian rupee. One rupee is made up of 100 cents, with note denominations of Rs25, Rs50, Rs100, Rs200, Rs500, Rs1,000 and Rs2,000 and coins of 5, 20 and 50 cents, and Rs1, Rs5 and Rs10.

### Foreign exchange and traveller's cheques

Foreign currency and traveller's cheques can be exchanged at the main banks, bureaux de change and larger hotels. As Mauritius is an ex-British colony, and British tourists are in the majority, pounds sterling are perhaps the best cash choice, but it is also easy to change dollars. Exchange rates are usually better in the country and at banks than at hotels, and no commission is charged for exchanging foreign cash, although there is a charge for traveller's cheques. The main banks on the island are the State Bank of Mauritius (SBM), Mauritius Commercial Bank (MCB), Barclays Bank, Hong Kong and Shanghai Bank (HSBC) and First City Bank. Although rates are similar between them, MCB is rumoured to have the quickest service. ATMs (automatic teller machines/cash machines) are widespread now in most towns, airports, large supermarkets and shopping malls.

### Credit cards

Major credit cards can be used at banks, most hotels, large shops and restaurants, with Visa and Mastercard the most widely accepted. It's worth checking if there's a charge, as some establishments add a 2–3 per cent processing fee. Cash advances on major credit cards are available from most of the main banks on presentation of your passport.

## Opening hours

Business hours are Monday to Friday 9am–4pm, and Saturday 9am–noon. Banks open Monday to Friday 9.15am–3.15pm, and Saturday 9.15am–11.15am; Post offices open Monday to Friday 8.15am–4pm, and

Saturday 8.15am–11.45am. Shops are open Monday to Saturday 9.30am–6pm; some open until midday on Sunday. Shops in Rose Hill, Curepipe and Quatre Bournes close on Thursday afternoon. Markets usually close around 4pm. Museums are generally open Monday to Sunday 9.30am–5pm, but are often closed on Tuesday or Wednesday. Check individual attractions' opening hours before setting out as there is no standard closing day in Mauritius.

## Passports and visas

Citizens from EU countries, Australia, Canada, New Zealand, South Africa and the USA don't need a visa to enter Mauritius and are permitted a stay for a period of two weeks to one month. All visitors need a passport valid for six months and a return or onward ticket.

## Pharmacies

Pharmacies are open in the evenings in most towns (look for the green cross) and well stocked with US and European medicines. There are dispensaries and health centres in most villages.

## Post

With over 90 post offices scattered throughout Mauritius, there should be no problems in finding one nearby. Letters are taken to the post office to post, rather than put in collection boxes. Most hotels will post letters or postcards for you. The postal service in Mauritius is quick and reasonably

reliable, with letters or postcards taking about a week to Europe and about ten days to Australia, South Africa and USA. A poste restante service is available at central post offices.

## Public holidays

Mauritius has 15 public holidays a year, although 8 are religious festivals where the dates change each year. These don't affect hotels, but attractions, banks and government buildings will be closed on these days. The seven fixed holidays are:

**1 Jan** – New Year's Day
**2 Jan** – New Year
**1 Feb** – Abolition of Slavery
**12 Mar** – National Day
**1 May** – Labour Day
**2 Nov** – Arrival of Indentured Labourers
**25 Dec** – Christmas Day

## Suggested reading
### Fiction

*A Smile of Fortune* and *Twixt Land and Sea* by Joseph Conrad are both set on the island.
*Paul et Virginie* by Bernadin de Saint Pierre is available in English.
*Le Sang de Anglais* and other books by Carl de Souza are set in Mauritius.

### Non-fiction

*The Dive Sites of Mauritius* by Alan Mountain (Struik, 1996). Comprehensive.
*Dodo – the Bird behind the Legend* by Alan Grihault (IPC Ltd, Mauritius,

2005). The definitive guide to Mauritius' most famous icon.

*Golden Bats and Pink Pigeons* by Gerald Durrell (Fountain, 1979). Informative and entertaining.

*Last Chance to See* by Douglas Adams and Mark Carwardine (Heinemann, London, 1990). Includes a good section on birds of the Mascarenes.

### Tax

Fifteen per cent value-added tax (VAT) is payable on goods and services, including hotel and restaurant bills, although hotels tend to include this in the price of rooms. In restaurants, a footnote will stipulate whether VAT is included or not. As Mauritius is a duty-free shopping centre, VAT paid on duty-free goods can be claimed back at the airport.

### Telephones

Public payphones using coins or pre-pay phone cards are installed

Tourist offices will help you find oddities like this temple on the southwest coast

throughout Mauritius, at bus stations, shopping centres or even in small corner shops, although they may not always work. Telecartes (phone cards) are indicated by stickers and samples of cards displayed in shop windows. These will include bookstores, supermarkets and news vendors or even fast-food snack bars in busy towns. Mauritius Telecom (*www.mauritiustelecom.com*) offers a good, reliable service, and payphones are found in their customer service centres in towns around the island. Of companies that offer pre-paid phone cards giving a much better rate for international calls, the most popular is Mauritius Telecoms Sesame. Others are Yellow or Allo; Cell Plus and Emtel cards are more expensive for international calls.

All large hotels and resorts will have international direct dialling, usually above the usual rate and sometimes extremely expensive. The country code for Mauritius from overseas is *230*. To make an international call from Mauritius simply dial *00* followed by the country code, for example:

Australia *00 61*
New Zealand *00 64*
South Africa *00 27*
UK *00 44*
USA and Canada *00 1*

Mauritius has good mobile phone coverage. Mobile networks use the European GSM system which means that you can activate a 'roaming' account if your phone is compatible. If you decide to rent a local mobile, local calls cost the same as from a landline. Contact your mobile provider for more details.

## Time

Mauritius is GMT + 4 hours in winter and GMT + 3 hours in British summer time. In the British winter, when it's noon in Mauritius it's 8am in London, 7pm in Sydney, 3am in New York and Toronto, and 10am in Johannesburg.

## Tipping

There are no rigid guidelines for tourists as to how much to tip for services, it's discretionary. Tipping is not expected, but appreciated.

## Toilets

Mauritius doesn't have an overgenerous provision of public toilets. You will find good ones at public beaches, attractions and in the newer shopping arcades. Otherwise, it's a friendly place, so try asking at cafés, hotels and restaurants.

## Tourist information

The Mauritius Tourism Promotion Authority (MTPA) has its head office and an information office on the 11th Floor of the Air Mauritius Building (*John Kennedy Street, Port Louis, Mauritius. Tel: 210 1545. www.mauritius.net*). There's a tourist information office on the ground floor. There is a surprising scarcity of tourist information offices around the island, but they can be found at Flic en Flac, Pamplemousses, Black River, Trou d'Eau Douce and at the airport. Free tourist booklets and leaflets produced by the MPTA include: 'Mauritius & Rodrigues information guide'; 'Rodrigues – your guide'; 'What's on in Mauritius' (annually); *Map of Port Louis & Mauritius*; and *Mauritius Green Map*.

## Travellers with disabilities

Many hotels claim to have facilities for people with disabilities, but some cater better than others. It's always best to check exactly what is offered before booking. Although main towns are accessible, some of the beach resorts have limited paving. Public transport doesn't cater well for travellers with disabilities, who may be forced to rely on tourist minibuses and taxis. Domaine les Pailles (*see p40*) is one attraction with full wheelchair access; a newly built conference centre and the Caudan Waterfront (*see p27*) are built with ramps and lifts, making some concessions to those with disabilities.

## Useful numbers

Airline departures/arrivals: *Tel: 603 3030*
Tourist information: *Tel: 152*
Tourist police: *Tel: 213 2818*
Directory enquiries: *Tel: 150*
Operator: *Tel: 10091*
International operator: *Tel: 10092*

# Language

Although English is the official language, Mauritian Creole (MC or Morisyen) dominates everyday life, and most people speak French too. In the tourist industry and in business circles, everyone speaks fluent English as well as other European languages such as Italian, German and Spanish. English is also used on traffic signs.

Most Creole words evolved from the pidgin French of the old plantation slaves, words like *liver* (winter) from the French *l'hiver*, and *dilo* (water) from the French *de l'eau*. Other languages have found their way into the mix – over 150 are derived from English, more than 50 from Indian languages, and several from Malagasy and Chinese. Mauritian people will be both surprised and pleased if you learn any Creole phrases, and it will help with bargaining in the market. Creole dictionaries such as *Parlez Creole/Speak Creole* by Rose Hill (Mauritius: Editions de L'Ocean Indien) are on sale in Mauritius. The following phrases (the Creole is spelled phonetically) will give you a headstart:

## PHRASES

| English | Creole | French |
| --- | --- | --- |
| Good morning | Bonzour | Bonjour |
| Goodbye | Bye/salam/ore revwar | Au revoir |
| How are you? | Kee Manyeer? | Comment ca va? |
| Are you okay? | Sava? | Est ce que ca va? |
| I'm okay, thank you | Bien mersi | Ca va bien, merci |
| Okay | Corek | D'accord |
| Please | Siupleh | S'il vous plait |
| Thank you | Mersi | Merci |
| My name is | Mo appel | Je m'appelle |

| English | Creole | French |
|---------|--------|--------|
| What is your name? | Coma oua peleh? | Comment vous appellez vous? |
| I want… | Mo ouleh… | Je veux… |
| Where is… | Cotte… | Où est… |
| I like… | Mo conton… | J'aime… |
| It's good | Le bon sa | C'est bon |
| How much is it? | Comyeh? | Combien? |
| It's expensive | Sai Sa | C'est cher |
| Market | Bazar | Le marché |
| Supermarket | Sipairmarseh | Supermarché |
| Chemist | La farmasi | La pharmacie |
| Post office | Le pos | Le bureau poste |
| Stamp | Teim | Timbre |
| Restaurant | Le restoran | Le restaurant |
| I'm hungry | Mofen | J'ai faim |
| I'm thirsty | Mo swaf | J'ai soif |
| Beer | La bier | La biere |
| Wine | Dee vin | Du vin |
| Tea with milk | Diteh avec dileh | Thé au lait |
| Waiters | Servair | Garçons |
| Hotel | Lotel | L'hôtel |
| Clean | Netwayeh | Nettoyer |
| Towel | Serviet | Serviette |
| I'm not well | Mo pas bien | Je ne sens pas bien |
| I need a doctor | Mo bisin en doktere | J'ai besoin d'un medicin |

## SLANG

| English | Creole |
|---------|--------|
| Very good | Vari bon sa |
| Hang out | Chakeh |
| Cool | Kul |

# Emergencies

## Emergency telephone numbers
Fire: *995*
Ambulance: *114*
Police: *999*
Weather information during
cyclones: *96*

## Health
Mauritius doesn't have malaria, and no vaccinations are required to visit. The most serious problem here is the danger of contracting Chikungunya, a viral disease transmitted by mosquitoes. Although the government are spraying to reduce breeding, visitors need to be liberal with the insect repellent to prevent biting, even in the day, and particularly in the warmer months (October–May). The only other problem may be an encounter with a pack of stray dogs, but rabies is not a risk here.

It's recommended you take out comprehensive travel and health insurance, particularly to cover any activities you want to do, and emergency repatriation cover if at risk of a serious illness. However, there is a good standard of health care in the private clinics across the island, which provide day-to-day medical services for a reasonable fee, and there is a couple of good public hospitals should you need them.

## Clinics
City Clinic, *Sir Edgar Laurent Street, Port Louis. Tel: 241 2951.*
Clinic Darné, *G Guibert Street, Floréal. Tel: 686 1477.*
Clinic du Nord, *Coast Road, Baie du Tombeau. Tel: 247 2532.*

## Hospitals
**Sir Seewoosagur Ramgoolam National Hospital**, *Pamplemousses. Tel: 243 3661.*
**Dr Jettoo Hospital**, *Volcy Pougnet Street, Port Louis. Tel: 212 3201.*

There are no poisonous reptiles or dangerous animals on the island. However, take precautions against the following sea creatures during your stay:
**Sea urchins:** Avoid walking on these as they are very hard to remove once embedded in your foot and can be infectious.
**Stone fish:** Although few are found on the island and hotels monitor their own beaches, this fish lies motionless and camouflaged on the sandy bottom of the sea. If you step on one, you should be treated urgently, as the venom can be fatal.
**Lionfish:** This distinctive-looking red and white, slow-moving fish has poisonous fins that it fans out and should not be touched.

## Crime and scams

Although Mauritius has a low crime rate, there is petty crime in the capital's crowded market and main tourist centre, Grand Baie. Break-ins to self-catering accommodation are not unknown, and lone women travellers should exercise caution and avoid walking alone at night. An unobtrusive tourist police operates in tourist zones to ensure the safety of visitors.

Follow the Mauritius Tourism Promotion Authority (MTPA) guidelines below to help ensure your safety and security on holiday:

● Keep an eye on all personal belongings at all times.
● Be careful when withdrawing money from a cash point.
● Avoid wearing expensive jewellery.
● Don't leave anything inside your car.
● For trips or purchases, use only recognised operators or suppliers.
● Keep your passports, plane tickets, jewellery and large sums of money in safes.
● During individual sea journeys, notify the person responsible for the boat.
● For sea excursions, don't rent boats with inadequate security standards.

### HOLIDAY HAIR TRANSPLANT?

The Hairgrafting Centre in Mauritius is one of the three most advanced clinics for this technique in the world and costs between 40–60 per cent less than in Europe.
*Centre medical de greffe de cheveux, Pointe aux Cannoniers. Tel: 269 0566. www.calvitie.net*

● Don't go swimming in areas where it is forbidden, clearly marked around the island.

Note that drug trafficking in Mauritius carries a heavy penalty. For the latest information on travel health and safety in Mauritius, check the Foreign & Commonwealth travel advice at *www.fco.gov.uk*

## Embassies and consulates

All embassies and consulates are situated in the capital, Port Louis.

### Australian Consulate
*2nd Floor, Rogers House, President John Kennedy Street. Tel: 208 1700.*

### British High Commission
*7th Floor, Les Cascades Building, Edith Cavell Street. Tel: 202 9400.*

### Canadian Consulate
*18 Jules Koenig Street. Tel: 212 5500.*

### New Zealand Consulate
*Anchor Building, Les Pailles. Tel: 286 4920*

### South African Consulate
*4th Floor BAI Building, Pope Hennessy Street. Tel: 212 6925.*

### US Embassy
*4th Floor, Rogers House, President John Kennedy Street. Tel: 202 4400.*

# Directory

## Accommodation price guide

Prices of accommodation are based on a double room per night for two people sharing, with breakfast.

| ★ | up to Rs3,000 |
| ★★ | Rs3,000–Rs8,000 |
| ★★★ | Rs8,000–Rs18,000 |
| ★★★★ | over Rs18,000 |

## Eating out price guide

Prices are based on an average three-course meal for one, without drinks.

| ★ | up to Rs300 |
| ★★ | Rs300–Rs700 |
| ★★★ | Rs700–Rs1,000 |

## NORTH

### Anse La Raie

**ACCOMMODATION**

**Paradise Cove Hotel & Spa ★★★**

Small, family-run hotel individually decorated in an Indian-romantic style. Dinner is in thatched huts on stilts over the lagoon. No young children allowed.
*Anse la Raie.
Tel: 204 4000. www. paradisecovehotel.com*

### Grand Baie

**ACCOMMODATION**

**Hôtel 20° Sud/Hotel 20° South ★★**

The first boutique hotel on Mauritius set in a quiet coconut grove on the waterfront facing Coin de Mire. Family run and good value for money.

*Route Côière, Pointe Malartic, Grand Baie. Tel: 255 1707/1715. Email: resa@20degreessud.com*

**Le Mauricia ★★**

This hotel provides excellent dining, land and water sports, a dive centre, a wellness centre and its own nightclub. Each room is sea-facing with a balcony. The Mauricia Village apartments are for families.
*Royal Road, Grand Baie. Tel: 209 1100. www. lemauricia-hotel.com.*

**EATING OUT**

**Le Capitaine ★**

Great seafood in a romantic setting.
*Coastal Road, Grand Baie. Tel: 263 7526. Open: Mon–Sat, lunch and dinner. Book ahead.*

**Don Camillo ★**

A well-priced, informal Italian restaurant.
*Coastal Road, Grand Baie. Tel: 263 8540.*

**Keg & Marlin ★**

English-style chain pub serving grills. There is also a branch at the Caudan Waterfront in Port Louis.
*La Salette Road, Grand Baie. Tel: 269 1571.*

**ENTERTAINMENT**

**The Banana Café**

A favourite frequented by tourists and locals. Live music ranges from R&B to Creole.
*Royal Road, Grand Baie. Tel: 263 8540.*

**La Playa**

The hottest bar in town, with a laid-back vibe.
*Kapu Kai Complex, Grand Baie.*

### Zanzibar Nightclub
A place to head for a good time after the bars and restaurants close.
*Royal Road, Grand Baie. Tel: 263 3265.*

#### SPORT AND LEISURE
### Croisières Australes
Catamaran cruises in Tamarin Bay, to Ile aux Cerfs and the Northern Islands.
*Coastal Road, Grand Baie. Tel: 263 1669. Email: cruise@c-australes.com*

### Grand Gaube
#### ACCOMMODATION
### Legends ★★★
The only hotel on the island designed according to feng shui principles. A wide range of water sports is offered, rooms are in bold colours and there's a great view across to the Northern Islands.
*Pointe Réjane, Grand Gaube. Tel: 204 9191. www.naiade.com*

#### SPORT AND LEISURE
### Yemaya Adventures
Led by previous cycling and kayaking champion, Patrick Haberland, Yemaya Adventures arranges mountain biking, sea-kayaking and hiking.
*Grand Gaube. Tel: 752 0046. www.yemayaadventures.com*

### Pointe aux Canonnier
#### ACCOMMODATION
### Le Canonnier Hotel ★★★
A 4-star hotel offering good-value, all-inclusive packages. It reopened in 2006 following refurbishment.
*Royal Road, Pointe aux Canonniers Tel: 209 7000. www.lecanonnier-hotel.com*

### Club Med ★★★
With Creole architecture, the hotel offers a host of activities from glass-bottom boat trips to waterskiing or sailing lessons. A great choice for active families.
*Pointe aux Canonniers. Tel: 209 1000. www.clubmed.com*

### Pointe aux Piments
#### ACCOMMODATION
### Le Méridien ★★★
A big hotel in a stunning setting on a lovely 800m (875yd) stretch of beach. All 198 large rooms and suites overlook the bay. As well as all the usual facilities, it has its own diving centre and shopping arcade.
*Village Hall Lane, Pointe aux Piments. Tel: 204 3333. http://mauritius.lemeridien.com*

### Le Victoria ★★★
Totally refurbished in 2006, Le Victoria offers half board at three restaurants, a large swimming pool close to the sea and plenty of water sports.
*Pointe aux Piments. Tel: 204 2000. www.levictoria-hotel.com*

#### SPORT AND LEISURE
### Exotic Cruise Ltd
Parasailing over the northern coast, from Grand Baie.
*Royal Road, Pointe aux Piments. Tel: 261 1724. www.catsails.com*

### Port Louis and surrounds
#### EATING OUT
### Le Café du Vieux Conseil ★
This is a popular spot for a Creole lunch in an open-air courtyard.
*Vieux Conseil Street. Tel: 211 0393. Open: for lunch only.*

**Namasté ★★**

An authentic Indian restaurant, with live music at the weekends.
*Caudan Waterfront. Tel: 211 6710. Open: Mon–Sat for lunch and dinner, Sun for dinner only. Book ahead.*

**Domaine les Pailles ★★/★★★**

Ten minutes' drive south of Port Louis, Domaine les Pailles offers a choice of four restaurants. La Dolce Vita Italian restaurant is the least expensive for lunch and has music at weekends (*Open: Wed, Fri & Sat for dinner*). The Indra, an Indian restaurant with live *tabla* music, is one of the island's best (*Closed: Sun*) and is more expensive. Other choices are Fu Xiao Chinese restaurant (*Closed: Sat lunch*), and Clos Saint Louis, which serves Mauritian lunches in a replica of a colonial home (*Closed: Sun*).
*Pailles. Tel: 286 4225. www.domainelespailles.net*

**Le Fangourin ★★**

The restaurant at L'Aventure du Sucre specialises in Seychellois fish dishes but also has good regional dishes.
*Beau Plan, Pamplemousses. Tel: 243 0660. www. aventuredusucre.com. Open: 9am–5pm.*

**Le Grand Casino du Domaine**

This is the nicest casino in Mauritius.
*Domaine les Pailles. Tel: 211 0452. Open: from 4.30pm; 7pm for tables.*

**The Palladium Nightclub**

Dance spot in a building made to resemble a Roman villa, on the road out of Port Louis.
*Trianon, near Port Louis. Tel: 454 6168.*

**Star Cinema**

Three-screen cinema showing Western films.
*Caudan Waterfront. Tel: 211 5361. Programmes: 11.30am, 1.30pm, 3.30pm, 6pm & 9pm, Fri and Sat also 11pm. Admission charge.*

**SPORT AND LEISURE**

**Les Ecuries du Domaine les Pailles**

Horse-riding for children over seven. Lessons too.

*Pailles. Tel: 286 4240. www. domainelespailles.net. Open: Mon–Fri from 7.30am.*

**Terre Rouge**

**ACCOMMODATION**

**Maritim Hotel Mauritius ★★★**

The stunning bar is a main feature of this vibrant hotel in 10ha (25 acres) of tropical gardens in Turtle Bay. It serves the island's most potent cocktails. The rooms are decked out in tropical colours, and the hotel also offers good snorkelling, a spa and a nine-hole golf course.
*Balaclava, Terre Rouge. Tel: 204 1000. www.maritim.com*

**Triolet**

**ACCOMMODATION**

**Trou aux Biches Hotel ★★★**

This tropical hotel with thatched and shingle-roofed bungalows shaded by palms on a long stretch of white, sandy beach is a firm favourite with families and couples. Nine-hole golf course and diving centre.

Trou aux Biches, Triolet.
Tel: 204 6565. www.
trouauxbiches-hotel.com

SPORT AND LEISURE
**Trou aux Biches Hotel**
A nine-hole par 32 golf
course.
Trou aux Biches, Triolet.
Tel: 204 6565. www.
trouauxbicheshotel.com.
Open: 7am–6pm.

# WEST
## Curepipe
SPORT AND LEISURE
**Vertical World**
Mountain climbing and
trekking.
Curepipe. Tel: 254 6607.
www.verticalworldltd.com

## Flic en Flac
ACCOMMODATION
**Villas Caroline ★★**
Small and recently
refurbished, this is an
unpretentious hotel on
its own beach with an
excellent dive centre.
Flic en Flac. Tel: 453 8411.
www.carolinegroup.com

**La Pirogue ★★★**
One of the oldest hotels
in Mauritius, La Pirogue
has had a recent
refurbishment but has
kept its uniqueness. One
of the best on the island
for families.

Wolmar, Flic en Flac.
Tel: 453 8441.
www.lapirogue.com

**The Sands Resort & Spa**
★★★
With 93 deluxe seafront
rooms and one suite, this
is a lovely, serene 3-star
hotel tucked away at the
quieter end of Flic en Flac.
Wolmar, Flic en Flac.
Tel: 403 1200.
www.thesands.info

**Sugar Beach Resort ★★★**
Grand colonial building
on the longest white-
sand beach on the island.
Wolmar, Flic en Flac.
Tel: 453 9090.
www.sugarbeachresort.mu

**Taj Exotica Hotel & Spa**
★★★★
Book into one of the
Taj's 57 luxury villas and
you're guaranteed 5-star
pampering in exquisite
surroundings. Think 24-
hour butler service,
plunge pool and giant
bed with great bathroom.
Wolmar, Flic en Flac.
Tel: 403 1500.
www.tajhotels.com

EATING OUT
**Domaine Anna
Restaurant ★★**
An unexpected find in
the middle of the sugar

fields, Domaine Anna is
open for lunch, but is
most spectacular at
dinner. Guests are greeted
with torches lit along the
drive, and groups can opt
for one of the gazebos on
the lakes. Live music and
dancing at weekends.
Médine, Flic en Flac.
Tel: 453 9650. Email:
domaineanna@intnet.mu.
Open: 10.30am–2.30pm
& 6.30–10.45pm.
Closed: Mon.

## Moka
ACCOMMODATION
**Eureka ★★**
The five peaceful guest
rooms facing the
mountain are set in
lovely gardens away from
the main house.
La Maison Creole, Eureka,
Moka. Tel: 433 8477.
www.maisoneureka.com

## Rivière Noire
SPORT AND LEISURE
**Le Ranch**
Experienced horse-riders
over 13 can join rides
through a privately
owned reserve.
Chemin Ramdenee,
Rivière Noire. Tel: 483
5478. Email:
charduc@intent.mu

**Otélair Ltée**

Mountain climbing and trekking.

*Tel: 696 6750.*
*www.otelair.com*

## Vacoas

**SPORT AND LEISURE**

**Gymkhana Club Golf Course**

The oldest 18-hole golf course on the island built in 1902 for the Royal Navy.

*Suffolk Road, Vacoas.*
*Tel: 696 2050. Email:*
*mgymclub@intnet.mu*

# SOUTHWEST

## Baie du Cap

**EATING OUT**

**Chand Restaurant ★**

This little yellow-painted restaurant with a spiral staircase is a real find for those on a budget. Catch of the day is usually your best bet and it's very cheap.

*Main Road, Baie du Cap.*
*Tel: 622 5827/760 3056*
*(mobile). Open: daily.*

## Bel Ombre

**ACCOMMODATION**

**Heritage Golf and Spa Resort ★★★**

A good 4 star in a new clutch of hotels, the

Heritage has an African-inspired spa, and warm, rich décor as well as an 18-hole golf course, kids' club, restaurants, tennis courts, and three pools.

*Bel Ombre. Tel: 266 9700.*
*www.veranda-resorts.com*

**Le Telfair Golf and Spa Resort ★★★**

Built in 2004, this hotel reflects the colonial grandeur of a Mauritius past. The spa is one of the best on the island, as is the golf course, and it has a kids' club, water sports, restaurants and a big pool. Guests share Chateau de Bel Ombre, a 19th-century house, with the Heritage Resort (see above).

*Bel Ombre. Tel: 601 5500.*
*www.letelfair.com*

**EATING OUT**

**Le Château de Bel Ombre ★★/★★★**

This elegant restaurant is in a beautifully restored building dating back to the early 1800s. There's a good-value prix fixe Mauritian lunch and à la carte dinner.

*Tel: 623 5620. www.*
*domainedebelombre.mu*

**ENTERTAINMENT**

**Shahrazad bar and nightclub**

With an Arabian motif and sheesha pipes scattered around, a good time is guaranteed.

*Voile d'Or Hotel, Bel*
*Ombre. Tel: 623 5000.*

**SPORT AND LEISURE**

**Golf du Chateau, Bel Ombre**

Built between the mountains and the sea, this challenging 18-hole golf course was designed by Peter Matkovitch. There are nine beginners holes.

*Le Telfair. Tel: 601 5500.*
*www.letelfair.com.*
*Heritage: Tel: 601 1500.*
*www.veranda-resorts.com.*
*Open: 7am–4pm.*

**Les Cerfs Volants**

Mountain climbing and trekking.

*St Felix Sugar Estate, east*
*of Bel Ombre. Tel: 212*
*5016 or 422 3117/3120*
*(mobiles).*
*www.lescerfsvolants.com*

## Chamarel

**ACCOMMODATION**

**Les Ecuries de la Vieille Cheminée ★**

Self-catering

accommodation in a 121ha (300-acre) estate. Guests stay in rustic Creole-style chalets with horse-riding, cycling and guided walks.
*Chamarel. Tel: 686 5027 or 725 5546.*
*www.ecuriecheminee.com*

**EATING OUT**
**Le Chamarel Restaurant ★★**
There are stunning views over Le Morne and Isle aux Béniters. Although it serves rather average Mauritian specialities, it's worth it for the view.
*La Crete, Chamarel.*
*Tel: 483 6421. Open: Mon–Sat for lunch. Book ahead.*

**Le Morne Peninsula**
**ACCOMMODATION**
**Indian Resort ★★★**
The Indian resort offers something for both action and relaxation in 11ha (4½ acres) of tropical gardens. The beach has kitesurfing at one end and a quiet beach at the other. The resort offers good value in a beautiful setting.
*Le Morne Peninsula.*
*Tel: 401 4200.*
*www.apavou-hotels.com*

**Dinarobin Hotel Golf & Spa ★★★★**
In front of Le Morne Mountain, this 172-suite hotel has arguably the most dramatic and romantic spot on the island. It also has a 7km (4 mile) white-sand beach and a wonderful Clarins spa.
*Le Morne Peninsula.*
*Tel: 401 4900.*
*www.dinarobin-hotel.com*

**EATING OUT**
**Le Verangue sur Morne ★★**
An open-sided lunch spot with wooden floor and tables as well as a stupendous view (ask for the corner balcony table). It has a prix fixe lunch and an imaginative à la carte menu, and optional helicopter arrival.
*Coeur Bois, near Le Morne. Tel: 483 6610.*
*Open: for lunch daily, dinner by reservation.*

**SPORT AND LEISURE**
**Club Mistral, Indian Resort**
Kitesurfing for beginners and advanced.
*Le Morne. Tel: 450 4112.*
*www.club-mistral.com*

**Yanature Adventures**
Mountain climbing and trekking with naturalist Yan de Maroussem.
*Tel: 785 6177.*
*www.yanature.com*

**Port Souillac**
**EATING OUT**
**Le Batelage ★**
In an old sugar mill on the mouth of a river, serving seafood specialities. Go on Saturday to catch a Sega (*see p16*) show.
*Village des Touristes, Port Souillac.*
*Tel: 625 6083. Email: lebatelage@intnet.mu.*
*Open: noon–5pm & 6pm–9.30pm. Dinner reservations required.*

**Rivière des Anguilles**
**ACCOMMODATION**
**Le Saint Aubin ★**
This is a chance to stay in a four-poster bed in your own wooden-shuttered colonial residence among birdsong in tropical gardens. Just two family rooms have access to a dining area, large veranda and small swimming pool.
*Rivière des Anguilles.*
*Tel: 626 1513.*

EATING OUT
**Le Saint Aubin** ★★
A quality Creole set table d'hôte lunch in elegant colonial surrounds with good service.
*See Accommodation p155.*

# EAST
**Belle Mare**
ACCOMMODATION
**La Palmeraie** ★★
Opened in 2006, La Palmeraie is in a good spot right on Belle Mare beach, near the elegant Residence Hotel. With a Moorish feel, this intimate 4-star hotel is both serene and different.
*Coastal Road, Belle Mare. Tel: 401 8500. www.hotel-palmeraie.com*
**Beau Rivage** ★★★
What's really unique about this hotel are its themed suites – Indian, African, Chinese – each is decorated exquisitely.
*Belle Mare. Tel: 402 2000. www.naiade.com*

EATING OUT
**Symon's Restaurant** ★
Offering a selection of Chinese, Indian Creole or seafood.
*Coastal Road, Belle Mare.*

*Tel. 415 1135. Open: 11am–midnight.*

SPORT AND LEISURE
**Legends and Links**
Legends has superb fairways in the heart of an indigenous forest. Links has rolling fairways and a signature 18th hole.
*Belle Mare Plage Golf Hotel and Casino Resort, Belle Mare. Tel: 402 2600. Email: headpro@ bellemareplagehotel.com. www.constancehotels.com*

**Post de Flacq**
ENTERTAINMENT
**Le Prince Maurice**
Blow the budget on the signature cocktail of perhaps the grandest hotel on the island.
*Poste de Flacq. Tel: 413 9100. www. princemaurice.com*

**Trou d'Eau Douce**
ACCOMMODATION
**One&Only Le Touessrok** ★★★★
Understated luxury on a spectacular site spread over three idyllic islands. A short boat ride away is Ile aux Cerfs Golf Course and Ilot Mangenie, a Robinson Crusoe-type

getaway. Dine on cuisines from eight countries at the excellent Three-Nine-Eight restaurant.
*Trou d'Eau Douce. Tel: 402 7400. http:// oneandonlyletouessrok.com*

EATING OUT
**Paul et Virginie** ★★
An elegant restaurant specialising in grills, seafood, pizzas and a variety of Mauritian dishes.
*Trou d'Eau Douce. Book through Le Touessrok Hotel. Tel: 402 7400. http:// oneandonlyletouessrok.com. Open: noon–3pm.*

SPORT AND LEISURE
**One&Only Le Touessrok Golf Course**
A course fringed by white sands and with a backdrop of green mountains sitting on a tropical island, this is voted one of the world's most stunning golf settings. Suitable for all players.
*Ile aux Cerfs. Tel: 402 7720. www.oneandonlyletouessrokgolf.com. Open: daily 6.30am–6pm.*

# SOUTHEAST

## Anse Jonchée

### ACCOMMODATION

**Ti Vilaz, Domaine du Chasseur ★★**

A collection of African-style thatched huts perched in this peaceful nature park atop the hill, with a stunning view to the sea. Don't forget the insect repellent!
*Anse Jonchée. Tel: 634 5011. www. domaineduchasseur.mu*

### EATING OUT

**Le Panoramour, Domaine du Chasseur ★★**

Perched 400m (1,312ft) up a hill, surrounded by green mountains and with a fantastic view of the southeast coast.
*Anse Jonchée. Tel: 634 5011. www. domaineduchasseur.mu. Open: 8am–4.30pm.*

## Blue Bay

### ACCOMMODATION

**Blue Lagoon ★★**

With friendly staff and all-inclusive packages, this 72-room hotel is a good-value option near the Blue Bay Marine Park and Mahébourg. It is only ten minutes' from the airport, so it suffers a bit from aeroplane noise.
*Blue Bay. Tel: 631 9046. www. bluelagoonbeachhotel.com*

**Shandrani ★★★**

On a double stretch of beach and within a 50ha (20-acre) garden. The Beachcomber's Sport and Nature ecotourism programme is based here. The only downside is that it is close to airport noise.
*Blue Bay. Tel: 603 4343. www.shandrani-hotel.com*

### SPORT AND LEISURE

**Beachcomber Sport & Nature**

Land and water sports can be arranged through this hotel.
*Shandrani Hotel, Blue Bay. Tel: 603 4540. www. beachcomber-hotels.com*

**The Shandrani Hotel**

This kitesurfing school opened in 2006.
*Blue Bay. Tel: 603 4343. www.shandrani-hotel.com*

## Cluny

### EATING OUT

**Le Val Nature Reserve ★**

Come here for the rustic atmosphere and the inexpensive lunch made from local fresh ingredients. Avoid the days when children crowd here.
*Near Cluny. Tel: 633 5051. Open: 9am–5pm. Best to book in advance.*

## Vieux Grand Port

### ACCOMMODATION

**Le Barachois ★**

With 16 rustic rooms of stone and thatch by the mangrove in a quiet corner of this coast, near the site of the historic battle of Grand Port.
*Anse Bambous, Vieux Grand Port. Tel: 634 5643. Email: le.barachois@yahoo.com*

### EATING OUT

**Le Barachois ★★**

A rustic stone restaurant with stick fences and thatch, coral underfoot and shells on the wall, Le Barachois specialises in giant shrimps, lobster and crab farmed here.
*Anse Bambous, Vieux Grand Port. Tel: 634 5643. Email: le.barachois@yahoo.com. Open: 9am–5pm for lunch. Booking necessary only for early dinner.*

# Index

# Acknowledgements

Limerick
County Library

Thanks most of all to Dad and Sara for their love and support and without whom I couldn't have made the guide happen. Thanks also to the MTPA, London, Toto Goorah and Reena, and in Mauritius Robin Ramhit and Mr Ramnauth; and hotel groups Beachcomber, One&Only, Naiade Resorts and all of the attractions to which I paid a visit. Thanks too to Karen Beaulah at Cambridge Publishing Management Ltd, for her patience and understanding. Thanks to Bob and Jackie Russell for their walking expertise; Bob Latimer for his diving knowledge; Amanda Statham for her honeymoon and spa expertise; Nicolas of Travel Designers (www.destination2mauritius.co.uk) those at the hash and the club who helped keep up my spirits and all those who helped along the way.

Thomas Cook Publishing wishes to thank the photographer, NICKI GRIHAULT, for the loan of the photographs reproduced in this book, to whom the copyright in the photographs belongs (except the following):
MTPA 4, 15, 23, 38, 115, 137, 140
www.bigfoto.com 88
ONE&ONLY RESORTS 16 (P. Tosselli), 34 (J. B. Adoue), 102 (P. Tosselli), 103 (P. Tosselli), 117 (Chris Tubbs), 126 (R. Starr), 136 (J. Nicholson)
YEMAYA ADVENTURES 107
BEACHCOMBER HOTELS 127

**Copy-editing:** JO OSBORN for CAMBRIDGE PUBLISHING MANAGEMENT LTD

**Index:** KAROLIN THOMAS

**Maps:** PC GRAPHICS, Old Woking, UK

**Proofreading:** JAN McCANN for CAMBRIDGE PUBLISHING MANAGEMENT LTD

# SEND YOUR THOUGHTS TO
# BOOKS@THOMASCOOK.COM

We're committed to providing the very best up-to-date information in our travel guides and constantly strive to make them as useful as they can be. You can help us to improve future editions by letting us have your feedback. If you've made a wonderful discovery on your travels that we don't already feature, if you'd like to inform us about recent changes to anything that we do include, or if you simply want to let us know your thoughts about this guidebook and how we can make it even better – we'd love to hear from you.

Send us ideas, discoveries and recommendations today and then look out for your valuable input in the next edition of this title. And, as an extra 'thank you' from Thomas Cook Publishing, you'll be automatically entered into our exciting monthly prize draw.

Emails to the above address, or letters to Travellers Project Editor, Thomas Cook Publishing, PO Box 227, Unit 18, Coningsby Road, Peterborough PE3 8SB, UK.

Please don't forget to let us know which title your feedback refers to!